INTRODUCTION

and

BIBLIOGRAPHY

INDEX

TO

MAIN FAMILIES, PERSONS, PLACES and SUBJECTS

=== IN ===

EGLE'S
NOTES AND QUERIES

INDICES OF THESE TWELVE VOLUMES

REVISED, REARRANGED, AND AUGMENTED

BY

MEMBERS OF THE STAFF OF THE PENNSYLVANIA STATE LIBRARY

With an Added

INTRODUCTION AND BIBLIOGRAPHY

By

A. Monroe Aurand, Jr.

CLEARFIELD

Published with the cooperation of the
Pennsylvania State Library

Introduction and Bibliography
Excerpted and reproduced with permission from
Notes and Queries:
A Bibliography (1934)
By A. Monroe Aurand, Jr.

GENEALOGICAL PUBLISHING COMPANY
BALTIMORE, 1970

Copyright © 1970
by Genealogical Publishing Company, Inc.
Baltimore, Maryland
All Rights Reserved.

Reprinted for
Clearfield Company, Inc. by
Genealogical Publishing Co., Inc.
Baltimore, Maryland
1993, 2005

Library of Congress Catalogue Card Number 70-114834
International Standard Book Number: 0-8063-4897-6

Made in the United States of America

INTRODUCTION

NOTES AND QUERIES:

Historical, Biographical and Genealogical

A Bibliographical Research

One of the most important fairly modern works dealing with the local, biographical and genealogical history of Pennsylvania, is that series of publications known as "Notes and Queries," edited by the late William Henry Egle, M. D., and contributed to by the best writers and students of Pennsylvania history from 1875 to 1900.

These contributions, which assembled form the "Notes and Queries," originally appeared in the Harrisburg (Pa.) "Daily Telegraph." The paper at that time was under the editorship of the late Mathias Wilson McAlarney.

It is fitting to pay proper respect to the memory as well as the efforts of Mr. McAlarney, who died December 5, 1900, less than three months before the death of Dr. Egle. We know of no better way than to quote from Dr. Egle's own words of tribute, as he addressed the meeting of the Dauphin County Historical Society, reported in the volume "In Memorium — M. W. McAlarney." (Harrisburg, 1901.)

Dr. Egle said, in part:

"No doubt it may be expected of me, owing to our intimate relations covering more than a quarter of a century, in announcing the death of our fellow-member, Mathias Wilson McAlarney, whose death occurred on the 5th of December, to say somewhat concerning that busy life which has passed out among the haunts of men. He came from good Scotch-Irish stock, and he was proud of it. The son of John McAlarney and his wife Catharine Wilson, he was born on the 7th of June, 1840, in Mifflinburg, Union County, Pa. He was educated at the public schools and at Bucknell University.

"He learned the 'art preservative of all arts,' in the printing office of C. N. Worden, editor of the 'Lewisburg Chronicle.' He read as

few do [from Mr. Worden's large library], the best of literary books,
gaining a fund of information. . . .

"In 1859 Mr. McAlarney went to Coudersport, Pa., and edited the
'Potter County Journal,' a weekly newspaper . . . . He took up the
study of law, and was admitted to the bar of Potter County, on February 27th, 1869. . . . In May following, he came to Harrisburg and
entered the practice of his profession. Here he became quite successful, but his taste was in the direction of editorial work, and from
1874 to the close of 1882 he was more or less actively engaged on the
'Harrisburg Telegraph.' In 1883 he purchased the controlling interest
in the Harrisburg Publishing Company, publishers of the 'Daily and
Semi-Weekly Telegraph,' and from that time on until his death was
the editor of the 'Telegraph' and manager of the company. . . .

"In 1887, [following interests that engaged his attention else-
where], he once more assumed active personal control of the Harrisburg Publishing Company, already referred to; and which establishment has wonderfully increased through his management. Few per-
sons have any idea of the large amount of work this establishment
has put out the last thirteen years. No other publishing house outside
of the very large cities has been so successful, and all through his
personal efforts and practical methods.

"To him we are greatly indebted for assisting in inaugurating
the plan of publishing in permanent and distinct form the valuable
and entertaining papers read before this society.

"In 1887 at Mr. McAlarney's earnest request, on leaving the
postoffice [the postmastership which he had enjoyed under several
presidents], your speaker continued the regular publication of 'Notes
and Queries,' the only condition being that all should be reproduced
in book form. He has always shown his appreciation of this valuable
series of historical, biographical papers, and his efforts along this
line have been rewarded. . . .

"After the Sesqui-Centennial of Paxton Church he was so interested in its success that he published a volume relating thereto——a
volume which is out of print, but treasured by all the descendants of
the early worshipers of that landmark of Scotch-Irish settlement.
The book contained everything then obtainable relating thereto.

"The Harrisburg Publishing Company has issued a large number
of historical and genealogical works the past ten years. Some of these
passed through his editorial supervision, and were made the more
accurate. . . ."

The death of Mr. McAlarney, in 1900, found a capable successor
to steer the "Telegraph" toward the goal of a century and more, of
usefulness. In 1883, when Mr. McAlarney acquired control of the
Harrisburg Publishing Company, there came to Harrisburg, from

Orbisonia, a young man just reached manhood—Edward J. Stackpole —fresh from the office of the Orbisonia "Dispatch."

Mr. Stackpole immediately became, as he says in his book, "Behind the Scenes with a Newspaper Man," (1927), "associated in a modest way with the Harrisburg 'Telegraph,' which I was destined to take over as owner and publisher in January, 1901. Thus my connection with the 'Telegraph,' as assistant foreman in the composing room, exchange editor, city editor, and finally, editor-in-chief and publisher, has continued for forty-three years."

The policy of Mr. McAlarney, in respect to the publishing of historical and legal, as well as military and other works of value, has been thoroughly carried out, and enlarged, by Mr. Stackpole, and his sons, Edward J., Jr., and Albert H., both active in editorial and managerial work. *

During the latter quarter of the nineteenth century, Harrisburg, central Pennsylvania, and the state at large for that matter, enjoyed the hey-day of historical interest and lasting evidence through the medium of printed books and periodicals.

The works such as accomplished through the initiative of Dr. Egle, and still others, whose published material came to an eager public through the well-known Lippincott Press, of Philadelphia, and a few other publishers, will stand as landmarks as long as they can stand the ravages of time, and the rough-handling of those moderns who care little for, and respect less, the efforts of men laboring but half a century ago.

Dr. Egle was, without a doubt, one of the foremost and most capable of all writers and students of Pennsylvania history. We are not unmindful of others who worked in similar fields of endeavor, such as Julius F. Sachse, Esq., and Prof. I. Daniel Rupp, and many others whose works are known far and wide, throughout the land.

While we have had the kindly cooperation of a number of librarians, scholars and students of history, it is well-nigh impossible to make a complete bibliography of all the "scraps" and the smaller contributions which can be attributed to Dr. Egle. In his day all the writing was done in long hand — letters, manuscript and the business of the day; that he must have been everlastingly at it, goes without fear of contradiction.

The mistakes which he made, (as are those of most of us), were unintentional; he can be forgiven for most of them; yet champions come forward from all directions to testify as to his ability. One says of Dr. Egle: "An unwearied delver after the history of the early

* The Harrisburg Publishing Company was reorganized in 1905, at that time becoming The Telegraph Printing Company. Today it has a modern commercial printing establishment, and a morning and an evening up-to-date newspaper.

times;" and from the well known Mr. Brock, of Virginia, we hear, "The accomplished editor."

Prefaces and acknowledgements, bibliographies and foot-notes, excerpts and quotations—all point to the importance of the works of Dr. Egle in the printed history of the State of Pennsylvania. We cannot do him too much honor in saying that the Commonwealth's history is many times richer because of him. County histories of all sorts, and many other books pay him, sometimes, all too little credit in their anxiety to shine brighter in light supposedly of their own making.

Dr. Egle was State Librarian for more than twelve years, having been appointed first by Governor Beaver, on March 3, 1887, and subsequently by Governors Pattison and Hastings. In this office he was of great service to his fellow men, of high or low degree.

His passing was actually and sincerely mourned by a great many people who had learned to love, and trust him. Rev. E. F. Smith, rector of St. Stephen's P. E. Church, in a sermon delivered on the Sunday following Dr. Egle's passing, the minister said, in part:

"William Henry Egle was a good and a great man. For once, there was no blind or empty compliment in the estimate the newspapers expressed of him. . . . The State is under great obligations to him for the results that he accomplished. . . ."

Students and others in search of historical data found their pathways widened and made brighter because of Dr. Egle, who found no little task too much to undertake; it seemed as though he found something new to interest him, in everything he undertook, no matter whether for himself, or for others. Thus, he found "pay dirt" day in and day out, because he lived not for himself, only.

While President of the Pennsylvania-German Society, in his annual address, page 17, volume III, of the Society's "Proceedings," Dr. Egle says: "When I was a boy . . . I made a scrap-book, the groundwork being some old copy books, and every clipping, odd, strange, and yet true, was carefully pasted therein. Twenty-five years after it made the reputation of a gentleman to whom I loaned it, and so I am reminded of the fact that had our ancestors kept memoranda of their industrious lives, of the recollections of the old home in the Fatherland, of the trials of pioneer life, its joys and its sorrows, the accurate records of their births, marriages, and burials, of removals to distant portions of the country — history, genealogy, and biography would have been an easy task, and we might all have the reputation of being historians and genealogists."

It is not to be supposed that Dr. Egle and his co-workers expected to make fortunes on their labors in the field of history and genealogy; rather it was the well-known labor of love, and pride in a rich heritage that drew these men on.

The Harrisburg Publishing Company, with Mr. McAlarney at its head, realized the importance of the work being conducted through its columns. Once a week, on Saturdays, for a period dating from 1884 to 1900, almost without a break, there appeared these all-illuminating articles on "old times" and "new."

There were also any number of well-worked-out genealogical lines, and a thousand and one other items of general interest.

During the early 1880's the articles appearing in the "Telegraph" found their way into pamphlet form covering much of what had appeared from time to time in the newspaper.

These pamphlets found much favor among the historians and others, and developed other contributors throughout the central part of the state, and, as time went on these issues became of extreme importance, and more or less difficult to obtain. Some of these "reprints" from the newspaper articles were limited to only 15 and 20 copies. Thus one immediately comes to the conclusion that such issues are difficult to find today — which is true.

In the course of fifteen years there appeared (1879-1894) a number of these "series" of "Notes and Queries," in pamphlet form, usually without date, so that it is difficult, even for the most apt scholar and student, to make either head or tail of these earlier issues.

Dr. Thomas M. Hams, Assistant to the Librarian, at the Henry E. Huntington Library and Art Gallery, San Marino, California, writes:

"We wish to complete our file of "Notes and Queries: Historical, biographical and genealogical:" edited by William H. Egle. We have been unable to find in any of our bibliographical works a complete description of this publication. We are listing the numbers we have, and if you can supply any of those missing, or advise which numbers are missing, we shall be glad to hear from you."

The foregoing letter was the straw that broke the camel's back, and this brochure, or monograph, with a detailed bibliography, is the result of such observations as passed before our vision. It has been carefully prepared for the limited number of libraries, genealogists and students who have recourse to the limited number of copies, or possibly sets, of this notable work.

A reading of this paper will help somewhat, those who have been otherwise unable to make some head or tail of the various editions and parts extant.

It was, and still is our intention, to point out that the original series of the "Notes and Queries" as reprinted from the "Telegraph" are almost as scarce as the files of the papers — with some reservations, of course.

For some years it has given us some concern as to the "gap" which we felt had occurred in "Notes and Queries," ostensibly sup-

plied by that other work of Dr. Egle's, known as the "Historical Register." It has never been made quite clear, but there was some reason for the "break," for the latter was issued from the establishment of Lane S. Hart, printer and binder; an entirely different source —one that would cost considerably more to operate than the former.

Now we are ready to prove what we had for a long time suspected—that Dr. Egle meant that the "Register" was to follow the Second Series of the "Notes and Queries," after its sudden conclusion in the "Telegraph" on Saturday, December 9, 1882. The pamphlet printing for the Second Series was not completed until early in the year 1883, which gave it that date, although the instalments were concluded in the paper in 1882.

Let us examine page 339, Second Series, (1883), and in the last instalment of the reprint of the same, the words of Dr. Egle:

"A Word to Our Readers.—At the suggestion of the present Editor of the 'Telegraph,' [Thos. F. Wilson], this number of 'Notes and Queries' as a regular publication will be the last. For almost four years, in sickness and in the hour of sorrow, we have endeavored to do our duty in the presentation of the history of this locality. There is yet much to be gleaned in that field, and some time in the future we may gather up a portion of what remaineth. Other localities call us, and the cessation of our labors in the present direction, enables us to pursue a course which we hope will meet with a proper and just appreciation — the establishment of a quarterly periodical devoted to the History, Biography and Genealogy of Interior Pennsylvania. Until the 'History of Dauphin County' upon which we are engaged shall have been completed, we will have no time to pursue local inquiry and research. With good wishes to our readers who have ever kindly received us, and to those who rendered assistance in our 'labor of love,' we bring our present line of work to a close."—[Harrisburg "Daily Telegraph," Saturday evening, December 9, 1882. — The end of the Second Series.]

There is evidence here in Dr. Egle's "valedictory" that he was "hurt" because his work could not go on.

In going over the files of the "Telegraph" we note that the paper did not carry any name at its mast head during 1882, other than "Chas. H. Bergner, Manager," until Friday, May 5, when the name "Thos. F. Wilson," appears as "editor." Perhaps it is merely a coincidence, but some excitement must have prevailed in the office on that date, due to the coming of the new editor, for the date line on the first page was the only one correct, the others throughout the paper being unchanged from the previous day!

Mr. Wilson continues as editor, with Mr. Bergner as manager, until October 28, 1882, when we note under the mast head, the following "notice:"

"Having disposed of all my shares in the capital stock of "The Harrisburg Publishing Company," my connection with the "Daily" and "Weekly Telegraph" newspaper and printing business ceased on and after the 1st inst.

"C. H. BERGNER."

This certainly makes it appear as though at the close of the year 1882, and just about six weeks before the last instalment of the "Notes," that there must have been a change in the policy of the paper, and that Dr. Egle was "persona non grata." Nevertheless, he takes hope again, as we see on page 77, volume I, of the "Register:"

"The title of this quarterly publication is sufficiently explanatory of our aim and object. We desire simply to preserve such information as from time to time may come to our hands, through the zeal and energy of others in connection with our own individual researches, of the history, biography, and genealogy of interior Pennsylvania. Of this data there is much to be gathered, and only so long as those gleaners in that field do not flag, but retain their interest therein, will this publication be continued. There is no reason why it cannot be permanently established, for there is much relating to the interior of our State, historically considered, which requires such a medium of inter-communication as the 'Historical Register' proposes to be."

The completion of the "Notes" in the "Telegraph" in December, 1882, was followed by the "Register," which was planned with the idea in mind, evidently, of carrying on with local history, perhaps even on a slightly larger scale. This is evident with the "Table of Contents," and the names and addresses of contributors, as well as the title pages, before us.

With the planning would also be a contract to issue quarterly, as Dr. Egle says, and once inaugurated, it was difficult to discontinue until the important articles had been concluded, for most likely the contributors were somewhat interested in the success of the stated quarterly—but perhaps not too much, financially.

In the Third Series, volume I, No. 1, for "July," 1884, more than a year after the last "part" of the Second Series had been issued, we read again the more or less "hopeful" words of Dr. Egle:

"To the Reader.—At the request of the Proprietor of the 'Telegraph,' [M. W. McAlarney], it is proposed to present in the Saturday's edition of that newspaper, all matters appertaining to the History, Biography and Genealogy of this locality. In recent researches much has come to light, while that which we had previously gathered, having been excluded by the publishers of the recent 'History of Dauphin and Lebanon Counties' from that volume, we propose to give the readers of the 'Telegraph.' Much is entirely new material, and all of it is valuable."

The above appeared in the "Weekly Telegraph," for January 9, 1884, more than a year since the last instalment of the Second Series, with Mr. McAlarney now the .dominant head of the publishing company.

In the early 1890's it was apparent to the local historians that the original series ought to be followed by a "reprint." This was agreed to by all concerned, among them a publisher who must have had a very generous heart, for there appeared in "1894" in an entirely new dress, improved and somewhat enlarged, the "reprint" of the "Notes and Queries."

The publisher plainly states in the "Prefatory to this Reprint," that "The papers contained in this limited edition [100 copies] originally appeared in the regular Saturday issue of the Harrisburg "Daily Telegraph" during the years 1878 to 1883. No contributions to any newspaper in the country have been so appreciated or more often referred to, and in a recently published Index to Local History pages of references are given to "Notes and Queries." To the student of American History, especially of that relating to Pennsylvania, this reprint will be invaluable."

This then, takes us to the very outset of the series. The publisher further states in the "Prefatory" that, "Owing to the increased interest at this time taken by the descendants of early settlers in Pennsylvania, and especially in Revolutionary ancestry, frequent demands have been made for the First and Second Series of the 'Notes and Queries.' Nearly one-third were never printed in pamphlet form, and except possibly in the possession of the Editor, no complete set of those are in existence."

In the reprint series, it may be stated "that all articles without signature were written by the editor, Dr. William H. Egle."

Basing our account on the few statements found in the "Prefatory" to the first reprints made, we readily see much that we cannot find easily, in the original papers, or the parts in which they appear after having been printed in the newspaper. All of this is due to the genuine scarcity of original numbers.

In a "Report of the State (Pa.) Librarian for the Year 1901," appeared a section devoted to "Bibliography of Pennsylvania," which was subsequently published as "Scotch-Irish Bibliography of Pennsylvania," and attributed to Major W. C. Armor, late of Harrisburg. This bibliography appears in several reports of Scotch-Irish Societies. As it appears in "The Scotch-Irish in America," Eighth Congress, 1892, and again in "Twenty-Seventh Annual Meeting and Banquet of the Pennsylvania Scotch-Irish Society" (1916), we reprint:

"NOTES AND QUERIES: Historical, Biographical and Genealogical. Edited by William Henry Egle, M. D. Harrisburg. 4to. Original series, 1879, pp 166. First series, 1881, pp 208. Second ser-

ies, 1883, pp 342. Third series, 1887, volume I, pp 588; 1891, volume II, pp 552; volume III, pp 565 [error: no volume III in the original series — Aurand]. Reprint, Harrisburg, 1894-96. Beyond all others the most important publication relating to the Scotch-Irish in America."

Inasmuch as the "Twenty-Seventh Annual Meeting" was held at the Bellevue-Stratford, Philadelphia, February 11th, 1916, some one overlooked a good opportunity for building up the bibliography of "Notes and Queries" to its fullness, for the last numbers appeared in 1900—more than fifteen years previous.

In our limited sphere of endeavor, even in the very city and heart of the field of operation of the late Dr. Egle, and his many able associates, we have been unable to uncover any original copies, or parts, of the so-called "Original Series 1879," numbering 166 pages.

There have been so many inquiries come to the present writer concerning this or that, in connection with this series of publications, that we are glad, once and for all, to lay these facts openly before those anxious to see the clearing up of the enigma of the parts of the original series, at any rate.

During the month of October, 1895, there appeared in the "Telegraph," the following ad:

"Early Series of Notes and Queries.— Owing to the frequent demands for copies of the Original, First and Second Series of 'Notes and Queries,' the Harrisburg Publishing Company proposes issuing a limited edition of the same for subscribers only. The Original Series was never printed in pamphlet form. These consisted of forty-two [forty-one] numbers. The First and Second Series owing to their exceeding rarity, are not obtainable at any price, there being not more than a dozen complete copies in existence. These being the repository of much data relating to the early history, biography and genealogy of the interior counties of Pennsylvania not elsewhere to be found, the proposition will undoubtedly be received with pleasure. The publication will comprise two quarto volumes of about 500 pages each, and the price fixed is $10 for the set."

In endeavoring to determine whether the "Original Series, 1879," was included in the reprints of the "First and Second Series," we have come to our conclusions through the mind of a printer and publisher, and sometimes bibliophile.

At page 291, First Series, reprint, we find instalment number XLII. We also find, in checking an original pamphlet, that No. I (1), of the original First Series, and No. XLII (42), of the reprint, start out with the same item, viz: "1001." The last insert of the original First Series is followed by the first instalment of the original Second Series, ("Shearman"), at page 63 of the reprint of the "First and Sec-

ond Series" volume II. This latter volume also concludes the same
as does the original volume of that same number.

Accordingly, the evidence then points to there being in the first
volume of the reprint series, some 291 pages of material which we
do not have some original pamphlet material to compare with.

The "First Series, 1881," according to the check we made, in-
cludes five pamphlets, for 208 pages. Of course, the number of pages
in the various series fluctuate, for they did the best they could in
those days of hand-set type, with no particular calculation on the ex-
act amount of space to be used. That an easy printing arrangement
was in force is apparent, for they printed but two pages at a time on
a job press.

The Congressional Library card on the early issues leaves much
to be desired, although they help the bibliophile, somewhat.

Going into the pagination, etc., of the "Third Series" reprint, we
quote again from the publishers' "Prefatory Note:"

"It is chiefly owing to the successful issue of the reprint of the
First and Second Series of the early issues of "Notes and Queries"
that a demand came for the continuation of the reprints. The Third
Series is just as valuable . . . and the few pamphlet copies that were
printed from newspaper type are extremely rare."

They also stated that "the Third Series will comprise three volumes." In the reprint it was three—in the original pamphlet series,
the Third Series comprised but two volumes.

The Original, the First, Second, Third, and Fourth Series were
printed from hand-set type, 7 or 8-point, solid or leaded. Many of
the letters and figures were much worn, some of them showing up but
faintly in the pamphlet printing. The Fourth Series, volume II, was
issued in 1894-1895. It concluded the "Notes and Queries" in
"series" form.

The reprint volumes, First and Second Series, volumes one and
two, and Third Series, in three volumes, were also in hand-set type,
10-point body, which accounted for the increase of one volume over
the number in the original series of the Third. The same was true
of the first two volumes being larger in the reprint, than in the original series; also due to the inclusion of the more or less obscure
"Original Series, 1879," in forty-one instalments, which accounted
for 291 pages of a total of 967 pages, (496, 471), in both First and
Second Series, volumes I and II, reprint.

The "Fourth Series," volume II, in hand-set type, appeared in
print only once. It was followed in short order by a reprinting of
volume I, from lino-type slugs. The original edition of volume II
bears the date 1893! Volume I, original edition, properly belongs to
the year 1893, but we are inclined to the idea that it was not actually

reprinted until after Nov., 1895, when linotypes made their first appearance in the "Telegraph" office. One doesn't set type by machine until one has a machine!

While the original Fourth Series, volume I, is dated "1893," it has a total of 428 pages; the reprint, with the date "1893," has but 328 pages! Care must be exercised when using the Index now available with reference of volume I, Fourth Series. The Index most generally seems to fit the reprint copy, with the 328 pages.

Following the "Fourth Series" there appeared annually for five years, dated "Notes and Queries," as follows: 1896, 1897, 1898, 1899 and 1900. This concluded the run of the most ambitious work of its kind ever undertaken in these parts, with the few pledges the editors and publishers had.

It must be said for the benefit of those who intend to use "Notes and Queries" for research, that after the type was used in the papers, it was held in the printing office until enough "matter" accumulated for the purpose of printing the sheets, or perhaps the convenience of those to whose lot it fell to do the actual press-work. In a number of cases, too numerous to mention at this moment, there were reprints of separate articles, either before, or perhaps after, the printing of the pamphlet parts.

The "salvage" process was frequently improved by corrections which were proved errors in the paper, or earlier numbers of the pamphlets. Some of these were noted weeks after publishing in pamphlet form. They might, or might not, show up in the original series pamphlets, but Dr. Egle, who was meticulous and painstaking, found use for his notes and corrections in the reprint series.

We find, that while the whole business was more or less a sort of catch-as-catch-can affair, when it was brought together in the reprint, it had the benefit of corrections, and even though articles were shifted around from instalment to instalment, most of those originally appearing, were improved in the reprint. Some, however, were not reprinted, and in course of time we may be able to determine what important items were omitted, and we may do our bit, by a reprinting of such as ought to be made more available.

Bear in mind that neither the First, Second, nor Third Series, original, had either "index" or "table of contents." The latter appeared for the first time in the series, in volumes I and II of the Fourth Series. The reprints are all improved with at least the "table."

It is not our purpose to go to any length in telling of the valuable contents of "Notes and Queries," except to say that the twelve volumes which comprise a complete set, encompass one of the richest stores of knowledge of Pennsylvania local history, biography, genealogy and many other items which come under the former subject indirectly. There is no substitute for this collection.

For many years it has been a hodge-podge of collected material, each volume of the reprints with a separate Table of Contents. Lately (1932), there has been issued a more or less comprehensive Index, or combined Table of Contents, developed by competent librarians and genealogists. It does not, however, claim to be a complete Index of "names."

The original edition of the "Notes and Queries" must have been very limited in number; the reprint we know has been limited to 100 copies. Many of these have gone back to the earth and light from whence they came, and others can be had—occasionally—from dealers, and, of course, an occasional auction.

Those wanting early church records, marriages, baptisms, deaths, graveyards, etc.; tax lists, early residents, and many other unusual and desired bits of information on central Pennsylvania, will do well to search these records.

A. Monroe Aurand, Jr.

NOTES AND QUERIES:

A Comprehensive Bibliography

The original "series" were issued "in parts," which we have carefully listed, and set forth as follows:

Original Series [1878-1879]

(Any items under this head must necessarily be in a limited number of scrap books.)

First Series [1880-1881]

Part	Instalment	First Words	Pages
1	[XLII]	1001 — In 1840	1- 40
		[Reprint says: "1810"]	
2	XLIX	Patterson, etc. 1-8; [41-48]	49- 80
III	LVIII (p. 85)	"Dutchland in America"	81-120
4	LXVIII (p. 130)	Contributions	121-164
V	LXXIV (p. 166)	Captain William Trent	165-208

Title page reads: "Harrisburg, Pa.: Telegraph Printing and Binding House, 1881."
No index; no table of contents; issued in parts.
The Part Numbers in the First Series are both Roman and Arabic, and we have used them as the original.

Second Series [1882-1883]

Part	Instalment	First Words	Pages
I	I	Shearman	1- 52
II	XIII	The First Letter	53- 92
III	XXIII	From Beyond	93-132
IV	XXXII	The Yorktown	133-172
V	XLI (p. 174)	Oliver Pollock (p. 173)	178-120 [220]
VI	LIII	(Cont'd) to Carlisle	221-260
VII	LXIII	Indian Burying	261-300
VIII	LXXIV	Vanlear	301-342

Title page reads: "Harrisburg, Pa.: Harrisburg Publishing Company, 1883."

No index; no table of contents; issued in parts.

In the "Index" published 1932, page 15, under "Egle 1883 1st. ed. 212, 213, 276:" this refers to pages in the original Second Series, the first page of which has pasted at the top of the first column, the line: "NOTES AND QUERIES. — I." The first word in the opening paragraph is "Shearman."

(Other examples using "1883 1st. ed." also mean "Second Series 1882-1883.)

Third Series [1884-1887]

Year	Vol.	No.	Instalment	First Words	Pages
1884	1	1	[I]	To Our Readers	1- 72
1884	1	2	XX	Heroes	73-144
1884	1	3	XXXVIII	A New Map	145-216
1885	1	4	LIII	Free Masons	217-288
1885	1	5	LXXIV (p. 292)	second Payment	289-360
1885	1	6	XCIII	McCann-Ebbcka	361-432
1886	1	7	CXII	Give Us Credit	433-520
1887	1	8	CXXVIII	Lehman Family	521-588

This last number contains the title page, "THIRD SERIES, Vol. I," with date line: Harrisburg, Pa.: The Daily Telegraph Print, 1887." No index; no table of contents; issued in parts.

Third Series [1887-1891]

Year	Vol.	No.	Instalment	First Words	Pages
1887	2	1	CXLVII	Rafting Fifty Years	1- 88
1887	2	2	CLXVI	Powell	89-172
1888	2	3	CXC	Jordan	173-244
1889	2	4	CCXVI	Rahm	245-308
1889	2	5	CCXXX	Lutheran	309-376
1890	2	6	CCXLIX	Mrs. Wentz	377-448
1890	2	7	CCLXIX (p. 451)	The First Census	449-552

Title page reads: "THIRD SERIES, Volume II. Harrisburg, Pa.: Harrisburg Publishing Company, 1891." No index; no table of contents; issued in parts.

Fourth Series [1891-1893]

Year	Vol.	No.	Mo.	Instalment	First Words	Pages
1891	1	1		I	[A New Series	1-104
1892	1	2		XXI	A Memorial	105-176
1892	1	3		XLI	Virginia Genealogies	177-232
1892[3]	1	4	Apr.	LV	The History	233-296
1892[3]	1	5	July	LXXIV	Diary	297-360
1893	1	6	Oct.	LXXXIX	Middle Ridge	361-428

Title page reads: "THIRD SERIES, Vol. II. Harrisburg, Pa.: Harrisburg Publishing Company, 1893." (Note: The "reprint" volume also has the same date on title page, but has only 328 pages).
Issued in parts; contains a "table of contents."
Example of indexing, as found in the "Index" (Table of Contents), published at Harrisburg, 1932:
> Bradford 1893 S4 I [page] 119
It is reasonably safe to assume that whether the date "1893" appears, or whether it is merely designated as "S4 I" [Series 4, Volume I], it generally refers to the reprint of Volume I, Fourth Series, 328 pages, and not to the original volume, containing 428 pages.

Fourth Series [1894-1895]

Year	Vol.	No.	Mo.	Instalment	First Words	Pages
1894	2	1	Jan.	CII	Coryell	1- 56
1894	2	2	Apr.	CXII	History of Sullivan Co.	57-116
1894	2	3	July	CXXI (p. 122)	Halifax Cent.	117-176
1894	2	4	Oct.	CXXXI	"Historical Journal"	177-240
1895	2	5	Jan.	CXLI	Revolutionary Soldiers	241-308
1895	2	6	Apr.	CLII (p. 4)	History of Sullivan County 1-24; [309-332]	333-365

Title page reads: "FOURTH SERIES, Volume II. Harrisburg, Pa.: Harrisburg Publishing Company, 1895."
Issued in parts; contains a "table of contents."

This concludes the "Original Series," printed from hand-set type saved from newspaper columns, and published more or less as

convenient. Annual volumes were printed from linotype slugs, for the years 1896, 1897, 1898, 1899 and 1900. These were printed but once, the concluding instalment having been published only about two weeks before the death of the able Dr. Egle, on February 19, 1901. The last instalment is his obituary.

Recapitulation of Original and Reprint Series

Originals				Reprints		
Series	Years	Pts.	Pp.	Series	Years	Pages
Original	1879	None		First and Second		
First	1881	5	208	v.I	1894	496
Second	1883	8	342	v.II	1895	471
Third v.I	1887	8	588	Third v.I	1895	560
Third v.II	1891	7	552	Third v.II	1896	496
Fourth v.I	1893	6	428	Third v.III	1896	565
Fourth v.II	1895	6	365	Fourth v.I	1893	328
Annual vol.	1896		239	Fourth v.II (no reprint)		
Annual vol.	1897		238			
Annual vol.	1898		308	(No reprints of Annual vols.)		
Annual vol.	1899		243			
Annual vol.	1900		237			

Historical Register

Volume I, 1883, in 4 parts   ....   318 pages
Volume II, 1884, in 4 parts   ....   318 pages

ABBREVIATIONS TO THE INDEX

S1-2	=	Series 1-2
S3	=	Series 3
S4	=	Series 4
AV	=	Annual Volume

Note: The series and annual volumes listed below are the volumes to which the references after each entry in this Index refer. The Index refers the user to the following volumes in the "Reprint Series" or the "Reprint Edition", and not the "Original Series" of these volumes:

Series 1-2, Volumes I and II

Series 3, Volumes I, II, and III

Series 4, Volume I

This concludes the "Reprint Series" or "Reprint Edition." It should be noted that the pagination, and in some cases the content, is different in the volumes of the "Reprint Series" or "Reprint Edition" from the pagination, and in some cases the content, of the "Original Series" and hence the Index can only be used for the "Reprint Series" or "Reprint Edition", not the "Original Series" of these volumes.

The following volumes are in the "Original Series", and they were printed but once:

Series 4, Volume II

Annual Volume, 1896

Annual Volume, 1897

Annual Volume, 1898

Annual Volume, 1899

Annual Volume, 1900

INDEX

HOW TO USE THIS INDEX

The user of this Index should first look at the page of Abbreviations which precedes the Index.

The Series Number (S1-2, S3, S4) or the Annual Volume Year (AV 1896, AV 1897, AV 1898, AV 1899, AV 1900) follows directly after each entry. In a Series reference, the individual volumes in that Series are indicated by Capital Roman Numerals (I, II, III), separated from the Series Number by a single space; the Page Number in the individual volumes are indicated by Arabic Numbers (1, 2, 3, etc.), separated from the Volume Number by a space. In an Annual Volume reference, the Year of the Annual Volume follows the abbreviation AV, separated from it by a space; the Page Number follows the Year, separated from it by a space. Thus, S3 I 74 is Series Three, Volume I, Page 74; and AV 1896 14 is Annual Volume for 1896, Page 14.

The page number given in the reference is, in most cases, the page where the material begins; page numbers hyphenated, as for example 234-236, indicate the material is on pages 234, 235, and 236.

A

Aborigines S1-2 I 420; S3 I 347; S3 II 401

Abraham, Noah S4 I 110

Ache S1-2 I 182

Achenbach Family AV 1898 232

Achey S1-2 I 182

Adamantine Guards S3 III 531

Adams, William J. AV 1896 217

Adams Family AV 1899 209

Addams, Robert S3 II 388

Africa, J. Simpson AV 1900 132

Agnew, John S3 II 422

Agnew, Samuel S1-2 II 201; S4 I 313

Agnew Family S3 III 289; S4 II 97

Agnew Family of Marsh Creek S3 II 28, 407, 426; AV 1899 61

Aigler Family AV 1899 185

Ainsworth, Samuel S1-2 I 317; S1-2 II 451

Alberdahn Family S3 II 221

Albert, Francis, Massacre of AV 1898 8

Albert, George Dallas AV 1898 252

Albert Family AV 1899 185

Albrecht Family AV 1898 47

Albright, Frances S1-2 II 202

Alcorn, James, notes S1-2 II 134

Alexander, John S3 III 67

Alexander, Oliver, inquiry concerning S1-2 II 293

Alexander Family S3 II 236; AV 1899 225

Alexander Family of Juniata
   Valley AV 1897 86
Alison, Dr. Benjamin AV 1899 91
Allabach, Colonel Peter H. S4 I
   83
Alleman Family S3 I 72; S4 I 32, 65
Alleman, Fencibles S4 II 147, 158
Allen, John Edward S4 II 195
Allen, Master, School of S3 I 36,
   51
Allen Family S3 I 1, 26; S3 II 377;
   S3 III 168, 220; AV 1900 51
Alliquippa, Queen S1-2 II 390, 432,
   460
Allison, Elizabeth Wilkins S4 I
   286
Allison, Robert, of Derry S1-2 II
   191, 206
Allison, William-1693 S3 III 206
Allison, William-1786 S3 I 27
Allison, Major William S3 I 2
Allison Family S3 II 141, 159, 464;
   S4 I 66; AV 1896 48
Allison Family of Derry S3 III
   164, 503
Allummapees, King of the Dela-
   wares S1-2 II 436, 460
Alricks, Hamilton S4 I 224
Alrick, Herman S1-2 II 203
Alrick, Hermanus S3 II 415
Alrick, James S1-2 I 317
Alter Family S3 I 521
Alward, Henry S1-2 I 14
American Patriot, newspaper
   S3 II 7
America's old wars S3 II 477
Anderson, Reverend James of
   Donegal S1-2 II 64; S3 I 380
Anderson, Captain Patrick S3
   III 58
Anderson Family S3 III 38, 269,
   366; S4 I 66; S4 II 257
Angst Family AV 1898 232
Antes, Henry-1784 S3 I 28

Antes, Henry-1818 AV 1899 76
Antes, Philip AV 1899 1
Antes Family AV 1898 222; AV
   1899 1
Anti-Masonic call S3 II 387
Anti-Masonic days S3 I 92; AV
   1896 146, 160
Anti-Masonic investigation S1-2 I
   152, 157
Antolhough, Manor of S3 II 91
Apple trees in the long ago S1-2 II
   183
Armolt Family S3 III 550
Armor, William C. AV 1897 110
Armstrong, Alfred S4 I 316
Armstrong, Dr. John S3 I 414, 530
Armstrong, Colonel John, letters
   of S3 III 465
Armstrong, Joseph, Jr. S3 III 207
Armstrong, Joseph, Sr. S3 III 206
Armstrong, Rebecca Lyon AV
   1898 126
Armstrong Family S1-2 II 422; S3
   I 8; S4 I 293; AV 1896 174; AV
   1898 167; AV 1900 16
Armstrong Valley, Bauerman's
   Church in S3 II 284, 288
Armstrong Valley, early settlers
   in S3 I 78
Army register of the U.S. from
   1775 to 1879 S1-2 II 30, 40
Arndt, Captain John AV 1897 170
Arnold, Benedict, treason of S3
   II 372; S4 I 98
Arnold Family AV 1899 185
Ashman Family S3 II 418
Askie Family AV 1900 34
Associators, the forerunners of
   the Pennsylvania line AV 1899
   97, 102
Aston Family S3 II 166; AV 1899
   54, 73
Atlee, Samuel John AV 1896 94
Atlee, Sarah Richardson S4 I 290

Atlee, William Augustus S1-2 I 146
Atlee Family S4 I 70
Attleman Family AV 1899 225
Auchmuty, Dr. Robert S1-2 I 203
Audenreid, Colonel Joseph C. S1-2 I 354
Auglaize, Battle of the S3 III 404
Aulenbach Family AV 1899 186
Avery, Benjamin Parke S1-2 II 92
Ayres Family S1-2 I 387

B

Babb, Samson AV 1896 205
Babb Family AV 1896 206
Bach Family AV 1898 234
Backenstose Family S4 I 120
Badges of the clans of Scotland S1-2 I 238
Baecker Family AV 1899 186
Bagwell Family S4 II 123
Bailey, Charles Lukens AV 1899 149
Bailey, Joel S1-2 II 204
Bailey Family S4 I 26
Baird Family S3 I 72; S4 I 149, 272, 300; AV 1896 203; AV 1898 167
Baker Family S3 II 247; AV 1898 167
Bald Eagle S3 III 488
Bald Eagle's Nest AV 1898 145
Baldridge Family S4 II 49
Baldy Family AV 1900 58
Ball, Thormond AV 1896 180
Ball Family S3 II 368; AV 1897 101
Ballie Family AV 1900 35
Balmer Family AV 1898 234, 235
Balsbaugh Family S1-2 II 373
Bangor Church, tombstone inscriptions AV 1898 61
Barbara Fritchie's Bible AV 1900 4

Barclay Family S3 II 137
Bard Family AV 1899 159
Barger Family S3 II 213
Bargman Family AV 1899 129
Barnett Family AV 1899 144; AV 1900 162
Barnitz Family S3 I 22
Barr Family AV 1899 172
Barrett Family S3 II 214
Barron Family AV 1899 189
Barth Family AV 1899 172
Bartlett Family S3 II 137
Bashore Family AV 1897 180
Batten Family AV 1898 230
Battin Family S4 II 275
Bauer Family AV 1899 186
Baum Family S3 II 24
Bauman Family S1-2 I 43; S3 II 232; AV 1899 173
Baumgartner Family AV 1898 232, 234
Bay, William F. AV 1898 292
Bayer Family AV 1898 233
Beader, Henry S3 I 28
Beader Family S3 III 550
Beale, Thomas S3 II 421
Beall Family AV 1897 123
Beatty, Reverend Charles S1-2 II 57
Beatty, George S1-2 I 318
Beatty, Captain James S1-2 I 457
Beatty Family S3 II 151; AV 1898 29
Beauchamp, Jacob S1-2 I 42; S4 I 171
Beaver, James A. S3 II 340
Beaver Family AV 1900 58
Bechtel Family AV 1899 186
Becker Family AV 1898 234
Bedford (Pennsylvania), tombstone records AV 1899 113, 118
Bedford County, militia, 1794-1796 S4 I 139, 158
Bedford Family S4 II 312

Bedford Presbyterian Church,
tombstone records AV 1899 113
Bedford Reformed Church, tomb-
stone records AV 1899 118
Beiser Family AV 1900 35
Beinhauer Family S3 I 73
Beissel, John Conrad, and his
disciples S3 I 284
Beizel Family S4 I 160
Bell, John, of Stony Creek AV
1898 71
Bell, Thomas, and family of S1-2
II 372
Bell Family S3 I 73; S3 III 162,
366, 494; S4 I 258; AV 1898 71,
167; AV 1900 173, 174, 223
Bellview Graveyard, tombstone
records AV 1898 43
Bender Family AV 1899 159
Benner, General Philip AV 1896
215
Bennett, James, early settlers on
the West Branch AV 1897 210
Bennett Family AV 1897 210
Bergner, Frederick Uhler AV
1896 145
Bergner, George S1-2 II 204
Berks County, Amity Church,
tombstone records AV 1897 207
Berks County, Oley Valley
Churches AV 1897 161; AV
1900 128
Berks County, Revolutionary sol-
diers in AV 1900 118
Berryhill, Alexander S1-2 I 131
Berryhill, Andrew S1-2 II 450
Berryhill Family S3 I 107; S3 II
400; AV 1899 231
Bertram, Reverend William S1-2
I 318
Bertram Family S4 II 234
Beula, a lost town S3 II 131
Beulah imprint AV 1900 159
Beverly, William S3 I 282

Beyer Family S3 II 220; S4 II 246;
AV 1899 186
Beyerly Family S3 III 532
Bible, an historic S1-2 I 452
Bibliographical threat S4 I 130
Bibliography S3 III 229; S4 I 164,
176; AV 1898 140, 171, 216, 220,
256; AV 1899 1, 25, 67, 116, 155,
156, 194; AV 1900 8, 91, 115, 205
Bi-Centennial celebration of the
landing of Penn in America S1-:
II 417, 451
Bickel Family S3 II 176; AV 1899
186
Bigler, William S3 II 335
Binckley Family AV 1899 173
Binder Family AV 1898 217
Bindnagel Church, records of S3
II 173, 181, 192, 206, 208, 219,
230, 290, 302, 308
Bindnagel Church, visit to S3 II
254
Bindnagel Family S3 II 213; AV
1898 232, 235
Bingham Family S4 I 79
Biographical data S3 II 5, 40, 48,
54, 69, 76, 97, 102, 260, 453, 462,
476; AV 1896 26, 43
Birkel Family AV 1898 232
Bird, James, the mournful tragedy
of (poem) S1-2 I 260
Bird Family S4 I 134; S4 II 152,
338
"Biscay Axes" of the Indian trad-
ers S1-2 II 208
Bishoff Family S3 II 64
Bishop Family S3 I 87
Bittinger Family S1-2 II 309, 337
Bizallion, Peter S1-2 I 153
Bizallion, Peter, grave of S1-2 II
216
Black, Andrew Krause AV 1897 54
Black, James AV 1896 180
Black, John AV 1896 180

Black, Reverend Samuel S3 I 380
Black, William S3 I 284
"Black Boys," an incident of the S3 III 271
Black Family AV 1896 76; AV 1899 32
Black Family of Derry S3 III 505
Black Horse Tavern S1-2 II 467
"Black Pete," Notice of S1-2 II 264
Bladen, Thomas S3 I 271
Blaine, James G., ancestry of S4 I 176
Blaine Family S3 III 175
Blair, Dr. Isaiah AV 1896 193
Blair Family S4 I 168; AV 1898 135
Blanchard Family AV 1897 12
Blasphemy, trail for S1-2 I 315
Blattenberger Family S3 I 88
Blecker Family AV 1897 34
Blessing Family AV 1898 234
"Blue Blood," inquiry concerning S3 I 3
Blunston's licenses S3 II 375, 380
Blythe, Benjamin S3 II 433
Blythe, Calvin, of Mifflin, note S1-2 II 191
Boal Family S3 II 213; AV 1896 26
Boas, Frederick-1784 S1-2 II 205
Boas, Frederick Krause-1815 S3 III 549
Boas, Jacob S1-2 II 205
Boehm Family AV 1898 174
Boesher Family AV 1898 235
Bogenreiff Family AV 1899 186
Boger Family AV 1898 234, 235
Boggs, John, note S4 I 110
Boggs Family S3 I 501; S4 I 108
Bohr Family AV 1898 233, 235
Bohre Family S3 II 248
Bollenbacher Family AV 1899 187
Bollinger Family S3 III 229; S4 I 100, 102

Boltz Family S3 II 219; AV 1898 232, 234
Bolz Family S3 II 210, 245
Bomberger Family S3 II 237, 245; S4 I 89
Bordner Family S3 I 388
Borst Family AV 1898 232
Bortner Family AV 1899 187
Boude Family S4 I 310
Bouquet, Colonel Henry, note S3 II 80
Bouquet's Redoubt S4 II 38, 177, 183
Bourdillon, Reverend Benedict S3 I 272
Bower Family S3 II 213; AV 1899 139
Bowersox Family AV 1899 166
Bowman, John F. S1-2 I 204
Bowman, John J., of Lykens Valley S4 I 148
Bowman, Wendel, deed to the land of S1-2 II 361
Bowman Family S1-2 I 43; S3 II 247
Boyd, Captain Adam S1-2 I 267; S4 I 312
Boyd, James Brisbin AV 1897 188
Boyd, Joseph S1-2 I 281
Boyd, Robert S3 III 434
Boyd, William S1-2 I 81; S3 I 28
Boyd Family of Danville AV 1897 25
Boyd Family of Lancaster and York Counties S4 I 66; AV 1896 142, 203
Boyd Family of Northumberland S3 III 190, 249, 434, 565; S3 II 228, 247, 475
Boyer, Weidner W. S4 I 129
Boyer Family S3 I 88
Bozart Family, old registry of S3 II 445
Bracken Family AV 1896 163

Brackenridge, H. H., anecdote of
S4 I 31
Brackenridge Family AV 1899 169
Braddock, monument to S4 II 67,
143
Braddock's Field, time of the
battle of AV 1897 63
Bradford, David, and Family of
AV 1898 128
Bradford, William, grave of AV
1896 7
Bradley Family S3 II 212
Brady, Captain John S1-2 I 123
Brady, Mary Quigley S4 I 296
Brady, Samuel-1734 AV 1896 20
Brady, Captain Samuel-1756 S3 III
272, 278, 285, 292, 300, 313, 322,
333, 340, 350; AV 1898 274
Brady Family S3 I 26; S3 II 213
Brainard's visit to Juniata Island
in 1745 S1-2 I 274
Brandon Family AV 1896 159
Brandstetter Family AV 1898 234
Brandt Family S3 I 88
Braun Family S3 II 233, 245; AV
1898 233
Brazington Family, inquiry con-
cerning AV 1900 121
Brecht Family AV 1897 141
Brechtbiel Family AV 1898 234,
235
Breckenridge Family S4 I 282
Breneisen Family AV 1898 233
Brenneman Bible AV 1896 33
Brenneman Family S4 I 69; S4 II
171
Brenner Family S3 III 428; S4 II
327
Bretz Family S3 I 35, 192; S3 II
283
Bright Family AV 1897 141
Brinkman Family S4 II 251
Brisban, Captain John S1-2 I 319,
352

Brisbin, Captain John AV 1899 93
British prisoners at Lancaster
S1-2 I 427; S1-2 II 354, 380; AV
1896 55
British prisoners at York S3 II 132
British prisoners in Pennsylvania
AV 1900 171
Brockden, Charles S3 II 378
Brodhead, Luke S3 III 491
Brodhead Family AV 1900 52
Brown, Eleanor S4 I 307
Brown, John, of Upper Paxtang
S1-2 I 18
Brown, John W. AV 1900 108
Brown, Dr. Mercer S1-2 I 319
Brown, William, of Paxtang S1-2
II 205
Brown, William, of Carlisle, note
S4 I 110
Brown, Captain William, company
of S1-2 I 483
Brown Family S3 I 12; AV 1898
232; AV 1899 201; AV 1900 70
Brown Family of Enniskillen S4 I
246
Brown Family of Fayette County
AV 1897 141
Brown Family of Mifflin County
S4 II 90
Browne Family S1-2 I 134
Brua, Peter S1-2 II 206
Brua Family AV 1900 189
Brubaker Family S4 I 95, 102, 113
Brule, Stephen, and his descent of
the Susquehanna S3 II 199
Bruner Family AV 1899 113, 126,
156, 161, 162
Brunner Family S3 II 231
Brunson Family S4 I 92
Bryan, John S1-2 I 291
Buchanan, John S3 III 356
Buchanan, Thomas S3 III 433
Buchanan Family S3 I 89; S3 II 15?
204; AV 1896 174

Bucher, John Conrad S1-2 II 391
Bucher, Reverend John Conrad
  S1-2 II 411; S3 I 432
Bucher, John Jacob S1-2 I 313
Bucher Family S3 I 542; S4 I 97;
  AV 1899 173
Bucher Family S4 II 222
"Buckshot War," S1-2 I 185; S1-2
  II 411
"Buckshot War," heroes of the S3
  I 177
Budden Family S4 II 123
Buehler, George S1-2 I 320
Buehler, Henry S1-2 I 247
Buffalo Crossroads Presbyterian
  Church, tombstones and rec-
  ords AV 1897 102
Bull, Henry S3 I 78
Bull, Mary Philips S4 I 272
Bull Family S3 III 162; S4 I 296
"Bumbo" and "Sangaree" S3 I 294
Bung, Peter S1-2 II 264
Burd, Colonel James S3 II 26; S4
  I 241
Burd, Colonel James, letters of
  S1-2 II 353; S3 I 527; S3 II 91,
  123; AV 1897 165
Burd, Colonel James, residence
  of S1-2 II 339
Burd, Joseph S. S4 I 98
Burd Family AV 1896 182
Burd Family of Tinian S3 III 231
Burd Farm S3 I 64
Burial place, an ancient S3 II 436
Burial places, destruction of AV
  1897 77
Buried treasure S3 III 553
Burnett, Augustus S3 I 411
Burnside, James S3 III 35
Burnside Family AV 1900 52
Burr, Aaron, meeting with Theo-
  dore Burr and General Hanna
  S1-2 I 197
Burr, Theodore, letter from, on

the construction of McCall's
  Ferry Bridge S1-2 II 142
Burr, Theodore, meeting with
  Aaron Burr and General Hanna
  S1-2 I 197
Burriett Family AV 1899 225
Burroughs Family S3 II 358, 369
Busch Family S4 I 160; AV 1898
  232, 234
Buser Family S4 II 250
Bush Family S3 III 403
Butler, Lord AV 1896 95
Butler, Captain Thomas, company
  of AV 1900 81
Butler, William, of Berks County
  AV 1896 200
Butler Family AV 1896 37; AV
  1898 159; AV 1899 230
Butler wills at Carlisle AV 1899
  230
Butterfield, Consul Willshire AV
  1899 177
"Buy a broom," (poem) AV 1896
  37
Buyers, John AV 1896 181
Byers, Frederick E. S4 I 300
Byers, John S3 II 416
Byers Family S3 II 429; S4 II 147

C

Cabell Family AV 1896 187
Caernarvon (Lancaster County),
  pioneer settlers in S3 III 79, 84
Caine Family S3 II 369
Calder, Reverend James S4 I 271
Calderwood, Captain James S1-2
  I 447
Caldwell Family S3 I 89; S4 I 4;
  AV 1898 252; AV 1900 86, 170
Calhoun Family S3 I 90; S3 II 214;
  AV 1898 89
California, the pioneer dentist of
  S1-2 II 441

Callahan Family AV 1897 175
Callender, Captain Robert S1-2 II
    76, 83
Callender Family S3 III 283; AV
    1900 91
Cambrian settlement S3 II 217
Cameron, John S1-2 II 392
Cameron, General Simon, letter
    of S3 III 398
Cameron School Building, dedica-
    tion of AV 1896 228
Cammerhoff, Bishop, journey to
    Shamokin in 1748 S1-2 II 237,
    243
Campbell, Francis, note S4 I 111
Campbell, James S1-2 II 134
Campbell, James, letter from S3
    I 536
Campbell, Lawrence, of Northum-
    berland AV 1899 113
Campbell, Colonel Thomas S3 III
    47, 550
Campbell Family S1-2 I 282, 385,
    419; S3 II 31, 248, 467; S3 III
    163, 254, 495, 550; S4 I 69; AV
    1900 7; AV 1896 142, 170
Campbellstown Evangelical Lu-
    theran Church records AV
    1898 132, 137, 147; AV 1899 227
Camp-meeting, early S1-2 II 422
Canal literature S4 II 331; AV
    1896 66
Cannassatego S3 I 289
Cannon Family AV 1899 14
Cantrill Family AV 1900 136
Capitol Building S1-2 I 281
Capitol Building, the first AV
    1896 225
Capitol Building, first chairs
    made for S1-2 II 77
Capitol Building, new laying of
    corner stone AV 1898 196
Capitol Clock, maker of the S3 I
    160

Capitol Hill in the long ago AV
    1897 60
Capp, John Charles S4 I 315
Capp Family AV 1896 155
Carl Family AV 1899 187
Carlisle, books published at S1-2
    II 71
Carlisle, distances from, to Lan-
    caster S1-2 II 294
Carlisle, distances from, to Pitts-
    burgh S1-2 II 71
Carlisle, tombstone records of
    persons born prior to 1800 AV
    1899 64, 69, 74, 80
"Carlisle Gazette" S3 II 198
Carlisle in 1806 S3 II 365
Carman Family S3 III 564
Carmany Family S3 II 183, 206
Carmichael Family S3 II 378
Carothers, John S4 I 111
Carothers Family S3 I 90; S3 III
    265; AV 1900 69, 214
Carpenter Family S3 III 550; AV
    1899 160
Carr Family S3 II 214
Carrighan Family AV 1898 235
Carruth Family, inquiry concern-
    ing S3 I 518
Carson, John S1-2 II 206
Carson, John, Family of S1-2 II
    313
Carson Family S3 II 349; S4 I 120;
    AV 1896 186; AV 1899 160; AV
    1900 195
Carter, Ezekial S1-2 II 392
Caruthers Family S4 II 186
Carver Family S3 II 433
Cassat Family S4 I 183
Cassatt Family AV 1900 190
Cassel, Margaret, of Dauphin
    County AV 1896 14
Cassel Family S4 I 88
Castle Family AV 1900 214
Cathay Family S3 I 514

Cathcart Family S3 II 79
Catherwood Family S3 I 514
Cathey, John S1-2 I 229
Catrell, William S1-2 II 393
Cattle, marketing of in 1755 S3 III 519
Cavet Family S1-2 II 390; S3 I 90; S3 II 476
Cavin Family AV 1896 187
Censors, council of 1784 S3 I 305
Centennial firms in Pennsylvania S4 I 179
Centre Hill Presbyterian Church AV 1897 221
"Century of dishonor" S1-2 II 57
Cessna Family AV 1899 204
Chamberlin Family AV 1896 187
Chambers, James AV 1896 191
Chambers, Joseph, note S1-2 II 305
Chambers, Katherine Hamilton AV 1898 227
Chambers, Maxwell, Family of S1-2 II 391
Chambers, Randle, administration account of S1-2 II 1
Chambers, Captain Stephen S1-2 I 485; AV 1896 171
Chambers Family S1-2 I 52, 80, 93, 189; S3 I 2; S3 II 202; S3 III 77; S4 I 109; AV 1896 191; AV 1900 126, 222
Chandler, B. Frank, note S3 II 108
Chapman Family AV 1899 209
Charlton Family AV 1899 188
Chartier, Martin S1-2 II 88
Chayne Family S3 II 378; S3 III 19
Chesney, William, note S1-2 I 114
Chesney Family AV 1896 187
Chester, Mrs. Jane S4 II 18
Chester, Colonel Lemuel S1-2 II 377
Chester, General T. Morris

S4 I 128
Chew, Benjamin S3 I 273
Childs Family AV 1898 235
Chillisquaque Presbyterian Church AV 1896 187
Chisolm, Judge W. W., assassination of AV 1896 199
Choir, a famous S4 I 319
Christie Family, inquiry concerning AV 1899 188
"Christly" an abbreviation for Christian S1-2 I 32
"Cider-Royal" S1-2 II 351, 366, 377
Civil War, a reminiscence of S3 I 437
Civil War, 36th Regiment, Pennsylvania, Volunteer Militia in S3 I 417
Clans, badges of the clans of Scotland S1-2 I 238
Clapham Family AV 1897 40
Clark, Elizabeth Jane S4 I 298
Clark Family S3 II 77, 215, 461; S3 III 37, 254, 262; AV 1896 167; AV 1899 138, 162; AV 1900 194
Clarke, James, of Indiana, note S1-2 II 188
Clarke, Captain John AV 1897 34
Clark's Valley, an early settler in S1-2 I 410, 436
Clearfield, first resident physician at AV 1897 129
Clearfield, tombstone records S4 I 123
Clemson Family S4 I 109
Clingan, Jane Roan S4 I 326
Clingan Family S4 I 109; S4 II 8; AV 1896 187
Clock, an old AV 1899 92
Clocks, old style S1-2 I 370
Clokey, Joseph S1-2 I 356
Cloud, William, deed for land on Paxtang S1-2 II 345

Cloyd Family, inquiry concerning
    S1-2 II 88
Clunie, James S1-2 I 320; S3 III
    95, 165
Clymer and Meredith estate AV
    1896 175
Coal, first used in locomotives
    S3 III 169
Coal trade, anthracite, chronology
    of the S3 II 7
Coal trade, Lykens Valley, devel-
    opment of S3 II 12
Coats of arms of Pennsylvania
    families S1-2 I 53, 216
Cobea Family S3 II 137
Cochran, William S1-2 I 321
Cochran Family AV 1900 70
Cogley Family S3 I 91, 440, 483
Coins, early American S1-2 II 309
Coleman, Dr. Samuel AV 1897 129
Coleman Family S4 I 97
"Colonial" or "Provincial" S3 II
    165
Colwell Family AV 1899 169
Compass (Pennsylvania), St. John's
    Cemetery, tombstone records
    AV 1899 15, 22, 25
Conestoga Indians S3 I 285
Conestogoe assessment for 1718
    S1-2 II 131
Conewago Burying Ground S3 II
    405
Conewago Falls Canal S1-2 I 191
Conewago Township, Dauphin Coun-
    ty S4 I 13
"Confab with Straw Jacket" S1-2 I
    242
Confederate Flag S4 I 93
Congress, "Colonial" or "Conti-
    nental" S3 I 355
Congress, first Pennsylvania elec-
    tion for S3 I 38
Connecticut intruders S3 III 472;
    S4 I 31

Conner, Commodore David S3 I
    104
Conner Family S3 II 400, 427
Connolly, Dr. John S4 II 148, 153
Connoway Family AV 1898 235
Conolly Family S3 II 119
Continental currency S3 II 227; S4
    I 25
Continental money, emissions of
    S3 III 104
Converse Family S4 II 259
Conyngham, Redmond, historical
    papers of S4 II 9, 20, 24, 27, 30,
    34, 36, 47, 54, 58, 64, 69, 74, 76,
    82, 91, 109, 111, 124, 125, 133,
    140
Cook, Martha Crawford S4 II 4
Cook Family S3 II 248; S4 I 69, 91,
    109; AV 1898 168
Cooke, Sarah Simpson S4 I 254
Cooke Family S3 I 7; S3 III 37; AV
    1896 180
Cookman, Reverend Alfred S3 III
    128
Cookman Family AV 1899 161
Cookson, Thomas S3 I 301
Cookson Family S1-2 II 428
Cooper Family S3 I 91; S3 II 284
Coover Family AV 1900 223
Cope Family S3 I 98
Coppenheffer, Captain Thomas,
    company of, in the Revolution
    S1-2 II 28
Corbett Family S3 II 214
Corbin, Margaret, note S3 III 555;
    S4 I 264
Cord Family AV 1900 69
Cormick's Plains, inquiry concern-
    ing S1-2 I 119
Corn in 1779 S3 I 476
Corran Family S4 I 96
Correll Family S4 II 245
Correspondence, old time AV 1898
    187

Corrigan Family S3 III 504
Cosine Family AV 1896 187
Coryell, Tunisen, reminiscences
    of S1-2 II 269
Coryell Family S4 II 1
Coulter Family S3 II 248
County Lieutenant, inquiry con-
    cerning the office of S1-2 II
    284
Courts, early manner of proceed-
    ings in S3 I 472, 478
Covenanters S3 III 236; AV 1897
    133
Covenanters, early, in Paxtang
    S1-2 I 20
Covenanters, first communion of
    S1-2 I 364
Covenhoven, Mary Kelsey Cutter
    S4 I 297
Covenhoven, Robert S4 I 118
Covode Family AV 1896 138
Cowden, Captain James, of Pax-
    tang S1-2 I 248
Cowden, Captain James, of Pax-
    tang, company of S1-2 I 259
Cox Family S3 III 165
Coxestown S1-2 II 277
Crabb Family S3 I 99
Craddock, Reverend Thomas S3 I
    271
Craig, Alexander S4 II 313
Craig, Isaac, letters of S1-2 I 133
Craig, Samuel S4 II 351
Craig Family S3 I 99; S3 II 138,
    377; S4 I 109; AV 1898 145; AV
    1900 52, 183
Craig Family of the "Irish settle-
    ment" AV 1899 238
Crain, Captain Ambrose S1-2 II
    393
Crain Family AV 1896 26
Crawford, George Addison S3 III
    545
Crawford, Hannah Vance S4 I 288

Crawford, Major James S4 I 142,
    144, 152
Crawford, Matty S1-2 I 140, 177
Crawford Family S1-2 II 100; S3
    II 297; S4 I 109, 142; AV 1897
    123, 198; AV 1899 172
Crawford Family of Hanover S1-2
    II 165
Creditors one hundred years ago
    S3 II 267
Creigh Family S4 I 211
Crewcorne Family AV 1900 47
Crider Family AV 1900 54
Criswell Family AV 1896 131
Crockett Family S3 I 99
Croghan, George S3 II 346
Croll Family S3 III 361
Crouch, Edward S1-2 II 211
Crouch, James S1-2 II 211
Crouch, Colonel James, residence
    of S1-2 II 339
Crouch Family S3 III 564
Culbertson, Alexander S3 III 356
Culbertson, Joseph S3 II 389
Culbertson, Robert S1-2 I 465
Culbertson, Samuel S4 I 110
Culbertson Family of Culvertson's
    Row S1-2 II 331
Cumberland County, early bar of
    S3 II 408
Cumberland County, Hanna's grave-
    yard, tombstone records AV
    1897 180
Cumberland County, records of
    slaves prior to 1790 S4 II 6
Cumberland County, Revolutionary
    heroes S1-2 II 422; AV 1900
    199, 210, 218, 224
Cumberland County, wills AV 1900
    69
Cumberland Valley, early settle-
    ment of S1-2 I 448, 486; S1-2 II
    82, 148, 155; S3 II 151, 279
Cumberland Valley, first road

through S1-2 I 447
Cumberland Valley, history of
S1-2 II 295
Cumberland Valley, marriages
AV 1898 214, 216, 229, 251; AV
1899 57, 58
Cumberland Valley, Scotch-Irish
settlers in S1-2 I 448
Cumberland Valley, soldiers in
the Revolutionary War AV 1900
199, 210, 218, 224
Cumberland Valley, tombstone
records in S3 III 450
Cumberland Valley, worthies S3
II 38, 413, 420; S3 III 206, 207,
214, 217, 222, 356, 413; AV 1896
43, 122
Cumberland Valley historical so-
ciety S1-2 I 1, 15, 358
Cummin Family S3 III 402
Cummings, John, note S4 I 77, 164
Cummings, Old "Billy" S1-2 II 242
Cunningham Family S3 I 99; S3 II
248; S4 I 109; AV 1897 2, 85, 91;
AV 1900 195
Currency in Dauphin County S1-2
II 170
Currency in Pennsylvania, anti-
Revolutionary S3 II 189
Curry, William AV 1896 192
Curry Family S3 I 309; AV 1896
192; AV 1899 224
Curtin, Andrew Gregg S3 II 337

D

Dale, Samuel AV 1896 101
Dale Family AV 1897 162
Dallas, A. J., letters of AV 1897
95
Dancing Club AV 1897 90
Danville, founder of AV 1897 97,
104
Danville Presbyterian Churchyard,

tombstone records AV 1897 11
Darby, William S1-2 I 33; AV 189
234
Dauphin (Pennsylvania) S1-2 I 267
S3 II 21
Dauphin (Pennsylvania) falling sta
in 1833 S3 II 20
Dauphin County, bar of, in 1789
S1-2 I 484
Dauphin County, first census of
S1-2 I 345
Dauphin County, first courthouse
of S3 I 200
Dauphin County, first prothonotar
of S3 I 445
Dauphin County, formation of S1-
I 412
Dauphin County, history of S1-2 I
Dauphin County, Huguenot settle-
ment in S1-2 I 202
Dauphin County, Londonderry as-
sessment in 1778 S1-2 II 55
Dauphin County, marriages in,
1793 to 1811 S1-2 I 182, 193,
198
Dauphin County, opposition to the
formation of S3 II 204
Dauphin County, Orphans' Court o
S1-2 II 296
Dauphin County, Paxtang and Mid-
dletown assessment in 1775
S1-2 II 15
Dauphin County, reminiscences of
S3 I 503
Dauphin County, "Upper End," ea
settlement of S3 I 462, 468; S3
282
Dauphin County, burials of, 1783
to 1810 S1-2 II 24, 35, 47, 123
Dauphin County, historical society
S1-2 II 52
Dauphin County, in 1789 S1-2 II 3
Dauphin County, in the Centennial
S3 I 244

Dauphin County in the Rebellion S3 I 417

Dauphin County in the Revolution S1-2 I 483; S3 I 417

Dauphin County in the Whiskey Insurrection S1-2 II 310

Dauphin County, names of places, origin of S1-2 II 13, 19

Dauphin County, population in 1800 S3 II 286; AV 1898 110

Dauphin County, settlers on Lake Erie S3 II 386

Dauphin County, tax collectors in 1782 S1-2 II 46

Dauphin County, taxables S3 I 16

Davidson, Catherine Martin AV 1896 102

Davidson, Samuel S3 II 410

Davidson Family AV 1899 107

Davies, Ann Schenck AV 1896 208

Davies, Squire John, letter of S3 I 382

Davies, Squire John, marriages by S3 I 385

Davies Family S3 III 99; S4 I 100, 151; AV 1899 144

Davis, David, "shop keeper at the Big Springs" AV 1897 169, 209, 231

Davis, Captain John, diary of, in the Revolution AV 1900 146, 152, 159

Davis, Adjutant John, orderly book of AV 1900 10

Davis Family S3 I 100; S4 I 97, 151; S4 II 142; AV 1897 169, 209, 231; AV 1899 148

Davis Family of Chester and Lancaster S3 III 52

Dawson Family AV 1899 216

Day of the month of the year S1-2 II 327

Dearmond, Richard S1-2 II 450

Deaths, early AV 1900 122; S3 II 476

Debating society, an old-time S1-2 I 80

DeBenneville, George AV 1898 103

DeBenneville Family AV 1898 181

Decoration Day S3 III 492

Deem Family S3 I 101

Defrance Family S4 I 229

Dehart Family AV 1900 34

Dehaven, John AV 1898 166

DeHuff Family S3 II 249

Deibler Family S3 I 78, 102

Deininger Family S3 II 182, 183, 184, 243; S3 III 381, 383

Delaware, trade boats on the, in 1754 S3 II 267

Delaware and Susquehanna companies S4 I 186

Delawares, Allummapees, king of the S1-2 II 436, 460

Delebaugh Family S3 I 101

Denny Family S3 II 257

Denning, blacksmith of the Revolution S1-2 I 190

Denter Family AV 1899 187

Dentler Family S3 I 101

Dentzel, John S1-2 II 212

Depui, Aaron S4 I 107

Derr Family AV 1899 61

Derry, Dunkard meeting house, tombstone records S3 I 84

Derry, East End assessment lists S1-2 I 115, 442

Derry, East End of, assessment lists, 1751 S3 II 22

Derry, East End of, assessment lists, 1755 S3 II 38

Derry, history of S3 I 319

Derry, Old Church at S1-2 II 435

Derry, original grant for S1-2 II 434

Derry, papers relating to S1-2 II 416

Derry, South End of, assessment

lists, 1757 S3 II 72
Derry, West End of, assessment
lists, 1751, 1755, 1757, 1759
S1-2 I 116, 400, 401; S3 II 17,
31, 88
Derry and Londonderry Township,
lines S1-2 II 136
Derry Church S1-2 II 435; S3 I 44;
AV 1900 65
Derry Church, admissions to S1-2
II 318; S3 I 155
Derry Church, baptismal records
of S3 I 140; AV 1898 53
Derry Church, deaths in S3 I 172
Derry Church, dismissions from
S3 I 165
Derry Church, graveyard wall at
S3 I 211
Derry Church, land patents of
1744 S1-2 II 5
Derry Church, last elder at S3 II
185
Derry Church, laying the corner-
stone of S3 I 315
Derry Church, marriages and
records of S3 I 137; AV 1898
54
Derry Church, original grant for
S1-2 II 434
Derry Church, relics of S1-2 II
100, 278
Derry Church, some mistatements
corrected S1-2 II 217
Derry Church, tombstone records
S3 I 75 (A-D), 80 (E-K), 93 (L-
M), 109 (N-R), 114 (S-W)
Derry Church records S4 I 235
Detch Family AV 1900 70
Detweiler Family S3 I 102
Deveny Family AV 1899 209
Devor Family AV 1899 152, 225
Dewart Family AV 1897 102
Dewees Family S4 I 110
Dewey Family AV 1899 76

Dewitt, Reverend William R. S1-2
I 321; AV 1899 109
Dewitt, Reverend William R.,
marriages by S3 II 473
Deyarmond Family S1-2 II 429;
S3 I 103; S3 III 235, 514
Dickey, Moses S1-2 I 250
Dickinson Presbyterian Graveyard,
tombstone records AV 1898 160
Dickson Family S3 II 203; AV
1900 69
Diebo Family AV 1899 187
Dieffenbach Family AV 1897 203
Dieter Family AV 1899 187
Dietrich Family S3 III 563
Diffebach Family S3 I 101
Dill Family AV 1896 143; AV 1897
68; AV 1899 139
Dilley Family AV 1899 225
Dillsburg Presbyterian Church,
tombstone records AV 1897 219
Dilworth Family S4 II 123
Dinwiddie Family S3 II 151
Disberry, Joe AV 1896 204
Dixon, Matthew Lyle S1-2 II 94
Dixon, Richard S1-2 I 81
Dixon Family S3 II 257; S3 III 428
Dock, Gilliard S4 II 269
Dock, William S1-2 II 212
Dock Family S1-2 II 404
Doctors and doctors' shops S3 I
23
Document, a curious S3 II 437
Dog-power grist mill S1-2 II 63,
77
Doll, Sarah McCallister S4 II 305
Donegal Church, roll of members
in, 1776 S4 I 182, 185, 189, 192,
196, 199, 202, 206, 207, 212, 214,
216, 218, 222, 228, 229, 236, 243
Donegal Presbytery members,
1732-1761 S1-2 II 170
Dorlan Family of Chester County
AV 1898 74

Dornbach Family AV 1899 187
Dougherty Family AV 1900 69
"Dough Faces" S3 II 172
Douglas, Samuel S1-2 I 322
Douglass Family S4 I 262; AV
   1896 158
Downey, John, educator and essay-
   ist S1-2 I 218; S3 II 221
Downey, John, letter of S3 III 200
Doyle, Peter S3 II 505
Doyle Family S3 II 166
"Drauss un Deheem" (poem) S4
   I 25
Dreisbach Family AV 1898 48
Drinks of our ancestors S3 II 424
Duane, William, 1760 S3 III 113
Duane, William, 1807 S1-2 II 452
Dubbendorff, Reverend Samuel
   S3 I 531
Duffield Family S1-2 II 219; S3
   II 257; AV 1899 148
Dunbar Family AV 1899 32
Duncan, Stephen AV 1898 151
Duncan, Stephen, of Cumberland
   County, note S1-2 II 190
Duncan, Thomas S1-2 I 485
Duncan Family S3 I 103; S3 II 201;
   AV 1899 148, 170, 225
Duncan's Island S1-2 I 234
Duncan's Island, in 1767 S1-2 II
   307
Dundore S1-2 I 2
Dunham Family AV 1899 225
Dunlap Family S3 I 26
Dunlop, James AV 1898 152
Dunlop, James, of Franklin, note
   S1-2 II 190
Dunlop Family S3 II 86
Dunning, Ezekiel S3 III 207
Dunning, Robert S3 III 208
Dunning Family S3 II 203; S3 III
   432
Durkee, John, note S1-2 II 305
"Dutchland in America" S1-2 I

391; S4 I 108
Dyre Family AV 1899 148

E

Earley Family S3 II 176, 206, 232,
   258, 291
Early, John, ninetieth birthday of
   AV 1896 151
Early, Martin, golden wedding of
   AV 1896 150
Early Family S3 II 265; AV 1897
   48; AV 1898 247; AV 1899 21,
   95
Eastburn, Benjamin, letter of
   S1-2 I 9
Eaton Family AV 1899 148
Ebbcka Family S3 II 64
Ebelhare Family AV 1899 160
Eberhardt Family AV 1898 236
Eberly Family S4 I 102
Eberman Family AV 1898 47
Ebersole Family S3 I 65
Ebersole Graveyard, tombstone
   records S3 I 500
Ebrecht Family S3 II 215
Eckstein Family S4 I 97
Ecroyd Family S4 II 162
Edgar Family S4 II 260
Edgell Family S3 I 476; S3 III 165
Edmonds, William S3 II 378; S3
   III 202, 537, 542
Education, early, in Pennsylvania
   S3 II 226
Edwards, Colonel Thomas S3 III
   560
Edwards Family S4 I 109, 151; AV
   1897 224; AV 1899 148
Ege Family S3 III 402
Egle, Beverly Waugh S1-2 II 383
Egle, Valentine S4 I 271
Egle, Dr. William Henry AV 1900
   227
Egypt Churchyard, tombstone

records AV 1898 74, 81, 86, 93
Ehrenfries, Joseph S1-2 II 394
Eicholtz Family S3 I 133
Elden Family, of Adams Co. AV
   1898 17
Elder, Jacob S1-2 II 394
Elder, Captain James, company of,
   in the Civil War S1-2 II 320
Elder, John S3 III 102
Elder, Reverend John, and the Pax-
   tang boys S1-2 I 434
Elder, Reverend John, correspon-
   dence of AV 1900 132
Elder, Reverend John, family
   record of S1-2 I 44
Elder, Reverend John, letter re-
   lating to the Paxtang boys S3 I
   330
Elder, Reverend John, marriages
   by S1-2 I 160
Elder, Reverend John, on "Long
   Bullets" S1-2 II 197
Elder, Reverend John, Paxtang
   and Derry's call to S1-2 I 16
Elder, Reverend John, sermon of
   S1-2 I 221
Elder, Joshua S1-2 I 323
Elder, Samuel, note S1-2 I 14
Elder Family AV 1897 46; AV
   1899 67, 167, 209
Eldred, Nathaniel B. S3 I 214
Eldred Family S4 II 320
Election muddle in 1777 AV 1896
   164
Eli Family S3 II 243
Elizabeth Furnace Estate, sketch
   of S3 III 224
Elizabethville Lutheran and Re-
   formed graveyards, tombstone
   records AV 1897 167
Elliot, James AV 1898 152
Elliot Family S3 II 152; AV 1897
   219
Ellis, William Coxe, of Lycoming,

note S1-2 II 190
Ellis Family S3 II 215
Ellmaker, Amos S1-2 I 323
Ely Family S3 II 237
Emanuel's Church at the Loop,
   records of AV 1898 23, 31, 108,
   112, 121
Emert Family AV 1899 187
Enders Family S3 I 4, 221, 388;
   S3 II 195; S4 I 113
Engel, Lieutenant Andrew, journal
   of, in 1757 AV 1897 13
Englebert, Anton F. S4 I 299
Ensminger Family S3 II 258
Enterline, John Michael S1-2 II 213
Enterline Family S3 I 229
Ephrata, Sharon House at S3 II 390
Ephrata Brethren, tombstone rec-
   ords AV 1896 67; AV 1899 173
Ephrata Cloisters S3 I 284
Epitaph, a queer AV 1897 176
Eppicher Family AV 1899 187
Ergelrecht Family AV 1898 236
Ernest Family AV 1899 187
Ernst Family S3 II 210
Eshelman Family S4 I 95
Eshenaur Family S3 I 133
Eshleman Family AV 1900 218
Espy, Professor James Pollard
   S3 III 73; AV 1897 215
Espy, Margaret P. AV 1897 215
Espy Family AV 1900 41, 42
"Estherton", alias Coxestown S1-2
   II 277
Etter Family AV 1898 236
Ettley Family S1-2 I 144
Ettwein, Reverend John, journal
   of, in 1772 AV 1898 49, 58, 68,
   77
Etzweiler Family S3 II 284
Euler Family AV 1899 187
Evangelical Annals AV 1900 182
Evans, Squire S1-2 II 182
Evans Family S4 II 283, 288, 296,

306, 315, 320, 329, 352; AV 1899
113, 126, 144, 157
Evans Family, of Delaware County S3 III 407, 414, 418, 426
Ewig Family AV 1899 187
Ewing, Reverend John S1-2 I 397
Ewing, Thomas, note S3 II 103
Ewing Family S3 I 552, 557; S3 II 103, 119, 258; S4 I 106; AV 1896 184; AV 1899 86
Executions in Pennsylvania AV 1900 190
Excise, collection of, in 1792 S1-2 II 334
Expedition from Fort Pitt to New Orleans in 1776 S3 III 421
Eyster, Jacob, 1786 S1-2 II 394
Eyster, Captain Jacob M., 1819 AV 1896 144
Eyster Family S3 I 4

F

Fager, John S1-2 II 213
Fager Family AV 1898 72
Fahnestock, Conrad S1-2 II 214
Fahnestock, Obed S1-2 I 324; S1-2 II 395
Fahnestock, William Eppley AV 1896 138
Fahnestock Family AV 1899 174
Fair at Halifax S1-2 I 311
Fairs, old-time S1-2 II 376; S3 I 169
Family graveyards, tombstone records AV 1899 231
Family records S1-2 I 273, 406
Farmer lad's day off fifty years ago AV 1896 161
Fast and Thanksgiving days in Pennsylvania S3 II 306
Fauss Family AV 1899 187
Fawcett Family S4 II 311
Federal Constitution, dates of

ratification S3 III 359
Federal Constitution, documents relating thereto S3 II 482
Federal Constitution, Pennsylvania's part therein S3 II 479
Federolff Family AV 1900 59
Fehler Family S4 I 120; AV 1899 187
Feiser Family S4 I 160
Fellenberg System of Education S3 I 151
Felty Family AV 1893 236
Fengel Family AV 1899 187
Ferguson and Graham Families S1-2 II 23
Ferree Family S4 I 66, 89
Ferries over the Susquehanna S1-2 I 106
Fertig Family S3 II 133; AV 1896 87
Fetterhoff, Philip S1-2 I 324
Fetterhoff Church records S3 I 538; S3 II 14
Fetterhoff Family S3 I 548
Fiedler Family AV 1899 187
Fiery Family AV 1899 129
Findlay, John S3 III 67
Findlay, William S3 II 331
Findley, William, note S3 III 460
Findley Family AV 1899 68
Fink, Henry AV 1898 15
Finley, Captain John S1-2 II 359
Finley, Margaret, note S1-2 I 59
Finley Family AV 1900 70
Finney Family AV 1900 100
Fire-proof buildings in 1810 S1-2 I 43
Fires, how formerly extinguished S1-2 I 86
Firnsler Family AV 1898 236
Fischel Family S4 I 160; S4 II 245
Fischer Family AV 1898 236; AV 1899 187
Fish, protection of, in 1792 S1-2

I 187
Fishburn Family S3 III 224
Fishburn Meeting House in Derry
AV 1896 120
Fisher, Emory A. AV 1900 109
Fisher, George S1-2 I 325
Fisher, George, will of S3 I 18
Fisher Family of Middletown
S3 I 424; S3 II 162; S3 III 549;
S4 II 306
Fisler Family AV 1896 119
Fithian, Philip Vicars S1-2 I 487
Flack Family S3 I 134
Flag, first American, in British
waters S1-2 I 452
Flag, history of the S3 II 211
Fleisher, John AV 1896 114
Fleisher Family AV 1896 127
Fleming, George, family of S1-2
II 372
Fleming, James S4 I 319
Fleming, Robert, in 1756 S1-2 I
325
Fleming, Robert Jackson, in 1803
S4 I 318
Fleming Family S3 I 135; S4 II
178
Flickinger Family S4 I 95
Flora Family S3 I 328; S3 II 258
Flueger Family S3 II 220
Foltz, Andrew AV 1898 15
Forney, John C. S4 II 135
Forney, Wien AV 1898 15
Forney Family S3 III 507
Forry Family S4 I 89
Forsch Family AV 1898 175
Forster, Allen, note S1-2 II 219
Forster, Arthur S3 III 217
Forster, John S1-2 I 327
Forster, Thomas (1st) S1-2 I 326
Forster, Thomas (2nd) S1-2 I 326;
S1-2 II 450; S3 II 402
Fort Granville AV 1896 174
Fort Hunter S1-2 I 415; S1-2 II

376; S3 I 4
Fort Lee, distance from AV 1900
194
"Fort Pitt" (block) S4 I 164, 176
Fort Pitt, distances from, to mouth
of the Ohio AV 1896 220
Fort Pitt, distances from, west-
ward S3 III 330
Fort Pitt, Indian Treaty at S3 III
347
Fort Pitt, treachery at S4 I 68
Fortune hunters S3 I 192; AV 1899
167
Foster, Hanna Blair S4 I 302
Foster Family S3 I 4; S3 II 138;
S3 III 77; AV 1898 28
Foulk, Stephen AV 1898 152
Foulke, Stephen S3 III 214
Foulke, William, vs. Goudy, Rob-
ert S3 II 412
Foulke Family S3 III 214
Fox Family S3 I 552; S3 II 78, 210,
244; AV 1898 236; AV 1899 187
Fox graveyard, tombstone records
S3 I 497
Fralich Family S3 I 135
France Family S3 I 135
France, threatened war with, in
1798 S1-2 II 138
Franciscus, Stophel, deed to the
land of S1-2 II 362
Franklin, Benjamin, and Lord
Howe AV 1900 196
Franklin, Benjamin, death of a
descendant of S1-2 II 452
Franklin, Benjamin, inquiry con-
cerning S4 I 178, 238
Franklin, Captain John, company
of, in 1780 AV 1898 85
Franklin, Walter S1-2 I 327
Franklin County S3 II 272
Franklin County in the War of
1812-1814 S1-2 I 448
Franks, Samuel D. S1-2 II 396

Frazer, Persifor S3 III 490
Frazer Family AV 1898 168; AV 1899 170
Frazier, John, note S1-2 II 305
Freck Family S3 II 283
Freeburg and its founder AV 1896 175
Freel, Hugh, tombstone record AV 1897 176
Freemasonry prior to the Revolution S1-2 I 256
Freemasons-Perseverance Lodge #2 AV 1897 194
Freemasons in 1796 S3 I 417
Freight charges in 1817 S3 III 41
Frembling Family AV 1899 214
French and Indian War, disbursements in S3 II 135
French and Indian War, muster-roll of S3 II 92
French and Indian War, note S3 II 125, 233
French and Indian War, soldiers in the AV 1896 220
French Family S1-2 I 120
"French Jacob" S1-2 I 42; S4 I 171
Frey Family S3 I 151; AV 1898 237
Freymeyer Family AV 1899 187
Fridley, Captain Jacob, company of S1-2 I 425
Friedenshuetten on the Susquehanna, Annals of AV 1897 199, 205, 211, 216, 221, 227, 233, 235
Friend Family, inquiry concerning AV 1897 8
Fries Family AV 1899 187
Frietchie, Barbara, her Bible AV 1900 4, 5
Fritchey Family S3 I 540, 542; S4 I 243
Froelich Family AV 1898 236
Frowert, Charles Edward S4 II 194

Fuchs (Fox) Family AV 1898 236
Fuess Family AV 1899 187
Fulton Family S1-2 I 2; S3 I 492; S3 II 259; S3 III 366; S4 I 88, 144, 170; S4 II 142, 157, 223, 335; AV 1899 170; AV 1900 178
Fundersmith Family S4 I 97
Funk, John, deed to the land of S1-2 II 362

G

Gainsburg S1-2 II 182
Galbraith, Andrew AV 1898 171
Galbraith, Colonel Bertram S1-2 II 349
Galbraith, Colonel Bertram, battalion S1-2 II 201
Galbraith, James S1-2 II 84, 295, 305
Galbraith, John S1-2 II 84, 87; S4 II 192
Galbraith Family S3 I 4; S4 I 136; AV 1898 72
Galbreath Family AV 1899 177
Gall, Ludwig Lambert S1-2 II 107, 116, 121
Gall, project of German settlements in Pennsylvania S1-2 II 110, 116
Gallitzin, Father S4 I 168
Garber Family AV 1899 44; AV 1900 195
Gardner Family S3 I 26
Garfield Family S1-2 I 403
Garrett, Major John, of Wyoming S4 I 250, 255
Garrett Family S4 II 317
Garrettson Family AV 1900 111
Garrigues Family AV 1899 159
Garver Family S4 I 120
Garverick Family S4 II 241
Gates Family AV 1898 48
Gawthrop Family AV 1900 51

Gebbert Family AV 1899 188
Geddes Family AV 1899 151
Geddes Family of Derry S3 III 197
Gehr Estate Contest S4 II 42
Gehr Family S4 I 88; AV 1899 188
Gehrhart Family AV 1899 188
Geiger, John L. S4 I 104
Geiger Family S3 II 139, 259; S4
  I 113; AV 1899 159
Geiss Family AV 1899 188
Gelbach Family AV 1900 35
Gelliger Family AV 1899 188
Genealogical memoranda AV 1896
  20
Genealogies, Pennsylvania S1-2 I
  145
Genealogy, the first, printed in
  America S3 III 229
Gensemer Family AV 1899 188
George Family AV 1899 148
Gerberich Family S3 II 231
German Exodus into England in
  1709 AV 1897 179
German Family AV 1898 240
German immigration AV 1900 217
German sects, defunct, in Penn-
  sylvania Die Gichtelianer AV
  1896 177
German sects, defunct, in Penn-
  sylvania, Die Inspiriten AV
  1896 173
German sects, defunct, in Penn-
  sylvania, Die Neugeborne AV
  1896 168
German sects, defunct, in Penn-
  sylvania, Dippels-Leute AV
  1896 179
German sects, defunct, in Pennsylvania, The Labadists AV
  1896 167
German sects, defunct, in Pennsylvania, The Quietists AV
  1896 178
German sects, defunct, in Penn-

sylvania, Rondoeriffer AV 1896
  172
German sects, defunct, in Penn-
  sylvania, Separatisten AV 1896
  177
German sects, defunct, in Pennsylvania, The Society of the Wo-
  man in the Wilderness AV 1896
  167
German sects, defunct, in Penn-
  sylvania, Zion's Bruder AV
  1896 173
Germans, English settlers' Con-
  tempt for S3 III 552
Gettig, Christopher AV 1896 203
Gettysburg, origin of name S3 III
  211
Ghost of 1776 S1-2 II 89
Ghosts of Swatara S1-2 II 367
Gibbons, William, letter of S1-2 I
  428
Gibbons Family S3 II 263
Gibson, Anne West S4 I 293
Gibson, Hugh, narrative of S3 I
  244
Gibson, John Bannister, chief jus-
  tice S1-2 I 338; S3 I 400; S3 II
  249
Gibson Family S4 I 62; AV 1898
  205
Gibson Family of Cumberland
  Valley S1-2 II 85
Gibson Family of Lancaster Coun-
  ty S3 I 244
Gilbert Family AV 1899 188
Gilchrist Family S3 I 213; S3 II
  263
Gildea, William Brown S1-2 II 441
Gillespy Family S3 I 136
Gilliland Family S3 II 138, 400
Gillmor, Moses S1-2 I 401; S4 I
  311
Gilston Family AV 1900 70
Gingrich Family S3 II 142, 259

Gintner Family S3 II 263
Girty, Simon, the "Tory Outlaw"
S1-2 II 66; S3 II 366
Girty, Simon, Sr. S3 I 1
Girty Family S3 II 412
Girty's Run S1-2 II 364
Gist, Captain, journal of
S3 II 430, 433
Gist, Christopher AV 1896 8
Gitter Family AV 1899 132
Given Family AV 1899 162
Glass Family S1-2 II 416
Gleim, Christian S1-2 I 328
Gleim, Colonel Harrison A. S3 III
363
Gleim Family AV 1900 156
Glentworth Family S4 II 29
Glidwell Family S4 II 256
Glossbrenner Family S3 III 192
Glover, William, note AV 1897
174
Gnadenhutten massacre AV 1899
232; AV 1900 86
Goebel, John Henry AV 1898 172
Goeckel Family AV 1898 240
Goods, how conveyed a half a cen-
tury ago S1-2 II 284
Gordon, George, of the Cumber-
land Valley S1-2 II 293
Gordon Family S1-2 II 71; AV
1898 168
Gorgas, Dr. Solomon R. S4 II 96
Gorgas, William R. S4 I 133
Gorgas Family AV 1899 174
Gottschall Family AV 1896 220
Goudy, Robert, vs. Foulke, Will-
iam S3 II 412
Governors' Mansions AV 1896 225
Governors of Pennsylvania, a cen-
tury of S3 II 329
Graeff Family AV 1898 45, 248;
AV 1900 52, 141
Graff Family S3 III 212; S4 I 89;
AV 1899 224

Graham, Reverend William S1-2 I
328; S3 III 247
Graham and Ferguson Families
S1-2 II 23
Graham Family S3 II 143; S3 III
88; AV 1897 131; AV 1898 1
Graham Family of Bedford County
AV 1899 21
Grant, Deborah Martin AV 1896
237
Graveyard, a neglected S3 II 112
Graveyard inscriptions, see
Tombstone records
Gray, Martin AV 1898 172
Gray, Robert, reminiscences S3
III 475
Gray, William S4 II 356
Gray, Captain William, pension
report of S3 III 83
Gray Family S3 II 260; S3 III 33
Graydon, Alexander S4 I 316
Graydon, Alexander, letter of
S1-2 II 385
Graydon, Hugh Murry AV 1900 45
Graydon, Rachel Marx S1-2 I 329,
339; S4 I 260
Graydon, William S1-2 I 331; S4 I
312
Grayson, William AV 1898 152
Green, Innis S1-2 I 330
Green, Colonel Timothy, battalion
in the Revolution S1-2 II 26,
45, 53
Green and Sterrett S1-2 II 46
Green Family S4 I 151
Greenawalt, Jacob AV 1898 41
Greenawalt, Major Theodore D.
AV 1897 33
Greenlee Family S3 II 215; AV
1900 69
Greer and Minshall, printers S1-2
II 107, 113, 122, 128
Greeg, William, of Paxtang S1-2 I
250

Greter Family AV 1899 191
Grever Family AV 1899 174
Grier Family AV 1899 62
Griffiths Family AV 1899 148
Groff Family AV 1900 141
Gross, Daniel Wiestling AV 1896
79
Gross Family S3 II 259; S4 I 120;
AV 1899 188
Ground-hog S4 I 93
Grubb Family S3 II 263; AV 1896
183
Gruber, Reverend Jacob S1-2 I
331
Gruber Family AV 1896 219; AV
1899 188, 190
Gueseman Family AV 1899 191
Gulliford Family AV 1898 168
Gump Family S4 I 160
Gurney, Francis S3 III 109
Gustine, Amos S3 III 412
Gutlender Family AV 1899 191
Gutman Family AV 1899 191
Guyasutha AV 1896 31

H

Haack Family AV 1899 191
Haas Family S3 III 548
Haass Family AV 1899 191
Haehnlen, Jacob F. S4 II 18
Haeny Family, inquiry concerning
AV 1899 152
Hagerstown, Maryland S1-2 I 489
Haldeman, Jacob M. S1-2 I 332
Haldeman Family S3 II 276; S3 III
556; S4 I 69
Halferty Family, inquiry concern-
ing AV 1899 152
Halifax, fair at S1-2 I 311
Halifax Election Riot of 1838 AV
1898 259
Halifax in 1824 S3 I 382
Halifax Centennial S4 II 117

Half-king or Seruniyattha S1-2 II
78
Hall, Dr. Henry S1-2 II 399
Hall, Louis William AV 1897 118
Hall Family S1-2 I 283; S3 I 401,
492, 494; S3 II 265, 276; S3 III
19
Haller Family S4 I 258; AV 1900
174
Halstead Family AV 1899 225
Haly, Mrs. Sara Haldeman S4 II
277
Hamaker Family S3 III 220
Hamborger Family AV 1899 191
Hambright, Captain John AV 1897
163
Hamill Family S4 I 188; AV 1899
209
Hamilton, Adam Boyd AV 1896 152
Hamilton, Hugh S1-2 I 332
Hamilton, John S3 III 97
Hamilton, Margaret Alexander
AV 1896 50
Hamilton Family S3 II 133; S3 III
1, 8, 13; S4 I 120, 293; AV 1896
43; AV 1898 135; AV 1900 43
Hammond Family AV 1896 198
Hand Family AV 1896 184
Hank Family S3 II 176
Hanna, General John Andre S1-2 I
484; S1-2 II 450; AV 1898 253
Hanna, General John Andre, meet-
ing with Aaron Burr and Theo-
dore Burr S1-2 I 197
Hanna Family AV 1898 60; AV
1899 155
Hannah Family S3 I 136; S4 I 66
Hanover, East, assessment lists
S1-2 I 83, 142, 351
Hanover, patriotism of S1-2 I 149,
405
Hanover, petition against division
in 1769 S1-2 I 85
Hanover, West, assessment lists

S1-2 I 143, 351, 404
Hanover assessment for the kings use, 1759 S1-2 II 209
Hanover Mennonite Church, tombstone records AV 1899 204
Hanover Presbyterian Church S3 I 53; S3 III 27; AV 1897 186; AV 1900 65
Hanover Presbyterian Church, tombstone records S3 III 261, 268, 271, 276, 284, 312, 344, 358, 362, 380, 386, 401
Hanover Presbyterian Church and Donegal Presbytery AV 1899 77
Hanover (Virginia), Presbyterian Congregation S1-2 II 198
Hanover spinster eighty years ago S1-2 I 140, 177
Hanover Township, original name of S3 I 221
Happel Family AV 1898 241
Harlow Family AV 1899 188
Harman, Joel, note S1-2 II 121, 126
Harper Family S3 I 136
Harris, David S1-2 I 133
Harris, Elizabeth McClure S1-2 I 333; AV 1898 288
Harris, Esther S1-2 I 9, 114
Harris, Henry L. AV 1898 195
Harris, John, and family of S1-2 I 42, 59, 160
Harris, John, events in the life of S3 I 505
Harris, John, grant of, to the town, county, and state AV 1896 207
Harris, John, in 1690 AV 1897 120
Harris, John, in 1753 S3 III 492
Harris, John, letters of S1-2 I 55, 258, 364, 390; S1-2 II 276; S3 I 200, 534; S3 II 46
Harris, John, "Recognance" of S1-2 II 267

Harris, John, Reeder's painting of AV 1900 36
Harris, John, rescuer of AV 1900 38
Harris, Robert S1-2 I 90; S1-2 II 450; S3 III 103
Harris, Dr. Robert, of the Revolution, tombstone record S3 II 368
Harris, Samuel AV 1896 218
Harris, Thomas, and his descendants S4 I 197, 201
Harris, William S3 III 492
Harris Family S3 I 7, 259, 332, 351, 372; S3 II 365, 466; S3 III 502; S4 I 27, 285; AV 1896 212; AV 1897 8; AV 1900 34
Harris Family in the Old Bominion S1-2 II 207
Harris Family of Paxtang S1-2 I 3
Harris' Ferry, affairs at S3 I 13
Harris' Ferry, border recollections of S3 I 544, 550
Harris' Ferry, declaration at S1-2 II 351
Harris' Ferry, "Feu-de-joie" at S1-2 II 230
Harris' Ferry, Whitfield at S3 I 387
Harris' Ferry to the Potomac in 1736 S1-2 II 292
Harris Mansion AV 1897 110
Harrisburg-Presqu' Isle Land Co. S1-2 II 443, 447, 453
Harrisburg, amateur theatricals at S3 I 92
Harrisburg, ancient hostelries at S1-2 II 123
Harrisburg, baptists of S3 I 70
Harrisburg, business men in 1800 S3 I 390
Harrisburg, deaths in, from 1800 to 1833 S3 I 160
Harrisburg, directory for 1839

S1-2 II 174
Harrisburg, early burgesses of
S1-2 I 267, 269; S3 II 39
Harrisburg, early churches in
S3 I 160
Harrisburg, early reminiscences
of S1-2 I 10; S3 I 553
Harrisburg, fires in S3 I 92, 168
Harrisburg, first bells in S1-2 II
314
Harrisburg, first grave-yard in
AV 1899 51
Harrisburg, first letter carrier at
S1-2 II 134, 147
Harrisburg, first newspaper ex-
plained (doggerel verse) S3 II
241
Harrisburg, first newspaper
printed in S3 II 239
Harrisburg, Hope Fire Company
of S1-2 I 158
Harrisburg, imprints S3 I 111,
542; S3 II 29
Harrisburg, inns of S1-2 I 297,
302; S3 I 71, 406; S3 III 39, 44,
49, 59, 65, 72; S4 I 96
Harrisburg, Jenny Lind at S4 I
152
Harrisburg, Lafayette in S3 II
493; S4 I 96
Harrisburg, last duel at S3 I 83
Harrisburg, latitude and longitude
of S1-2 II 404
Harrisburg, lot book of John Har-
ris S1-2 II 96
Harrisburg, magnetic telegraph
first at S1-2 I 253
Harrisburg, magnetic telegraph
office at S1-2 I 257
Harrisburg, mails for, in 1798
S1-2 II 241
Harrisburg, manners and customs
S3 I 22, 66, 79, 96, 225
Harrisburg, manufacturing facili-
ties of S1-2 I 346
Harrisburg, Market Square at S3
III 307; AV 1899 28, 33
Harrisburg, markets in early days
of S1-2 II 398
Harrisburg, military school at
S1-2 I 61, 72, 84
Harrisburg, Mill Dam, troubles at
S3 II 9
Harrisburg, Mount Joy and Lan-
caster R. R., opening of S4 I 18
Harrisburg, municipal officers of
S3 II 41
Harrisburg, North Ward School in
1844 S4 I 77
Harrisburg, note S3 II 106
Harrisburg, old band of AV 1900
110
Harrisburg, old bridge at AV 1899
39
Harrisburg, original name of S1-2
I 418
Harrisburg, Orphan Asylum at
S1-2 II 423
Harrisburg, population of, in 1810
and 1820 S3 I 184
Harrisburg, Post Office, location
of S1-2 I 51
Harrisburg, postmasters of S1-2
I 46, 51, 411
Harrisburg, President Washing-
ton's visit to S1-2 II 52
Harrisburg, railroad cars first at
S1-2 I 460
Harrisburg, railroad stations at
S3 I 128
Harrisburg, reminiscences of S3
III 212; AV 1898 6, 34; AV 1899
182; AV 1900 16, 59, 65, 92
Harrisburg, ride from Shank's Hil
to S3 III 19
Harrisburg, "The Riffles" at AV
1900 178
Harrisburg, street regulators

S3 I 406
Harrisburg Board of Health S3 I
191
Harrisburg from 1828 to 1840 S3
III 444, 447, 453
Harrisburg in 1784 S1-2 I 441
Harrisburg in 1785 S3 I 389; AV
1896 130
Harrisburg in 1787 S1-2 I 120
Harrisburg in 1792-3 S1-2 II 96,
102
Harrisburg in 1794 S1-2 I 6
Harrisburg in 1797 S3 II 179
Harrisburg in 1818 S1-2 I 405
Harrisburg in 1819 S1-2 II 109
Harrisburg in 1820 S3 II 366
Harrisburg in 1828 S1-2 I 244
Harrisburg in 1841 S3 III 311
Harrisburg in the War of 1812-
1814 S1-2 I 280
Harrisburg German Society of
1820 S1-2 II 117
Harrisburg to Middletown, remin-
iscences of S4 II 78
Harrison, General John S1-2 I 32;
S1-2 II 214
Harrison Family S3 II 74, 215; S3
III 179, 307, 518
Hart, Gustavus N. AV 1899 55,
147, 152
Hart Family S4 I 100
Hartlein Family AV 1898 175
Hartley, Katherine Holtzinger AV
1896 49
Hartzler Family AV 1899 102
Harvey Book, the AV 1900 91
Hatz Family AV 1898 240
Hauk Family AV 1898 174
Hause Family S3 III 416
Hayden, Reverend Thomas S1-2 II
297
Hayes Family S1-2 II 159; S3 II
264, 276; S4 I 215
Hayes Family of Derry S1-2 II 159

Hays, Anna Margaret S4 I 83
Hays, Mary Ludwig S3 I 265
Hays, Samuel Wallace S4 I 317
Hays Family of Northampton Coun-
ty AV 1899 116, 189
Hazlett Family AV 1900 42
Hebel, George S1-2 II 337
Hebker Family S3 I 518
Hebron Church diary, 1775-1783
S4 II 332, 341, 347, 353, 356
Hebron Church marriage records
S1-2 I 461; S4 I 16
Heckendorn Family S4 I 159; S4 II
246, 251
Heckert Family S3 I 152
Heckman's Church of Penn's Val-
ley, Pennsylvania AV 1900 195
Hedderich Family AV 1899 191
Hederich Family AV 1898 240
Hehl Family AV 1898 46
Heidelberg Tax List for 1758 AV
1898 18
Heiliger Family AV 1899 191
Heinrich Family AV 1894 191
Heisely, Frederick S1-2 II 400
Hemperly Family S3 I 152; S3 II
182, 183, 194; AV 1898 240
Hemphill Family AV 1899 170
Henderson, Dr. William B. AV
1896 227
Henderson Family S3 I 136; S4 II
316; AV 1898 96
Hendricks, Tobias, note S1-2 II 88
Hendricks, Captain William, com-
pany of S1-2 I 450
Hendricks Family S3 II 264; AV
1896 31; AV 1899 177
Henry, Ann Wood S4 I 284
Henry, John Joseph S1-2 I 485
Henry, John Joseph, burial place
of S3 III 368
Henry Family S3 I 127; S3 II 237;
S4 I 95; AV 1896 125; AV 1898
46

Henry Family of Spring Creek S4
I 2
Hepburn, Andrew D. AV 1897 146
Hepburn, Creoy Covenhoven S4 I
294
Hepburn, James AV 1897 142
Hepburn, Samuel AV 1897 24
Hepburn, Judge William AV 1897
166
Hepburn Family AV 1897 24, 142,
146
Heraldic Arms of Pennsylvania
families S1-2 I 53, 216
Herbster Family AV 1898 240
Herculaneum MSS., inquiry con-
cerning S1-2 I 281
Hercules, rescuer of John Harris
AV 1900 38
Heroes, heavy weighted S3 II 164
Herr, Andrew Jackson S4 II 16
Herr, Christian, deed to the land
of S1-2 II 361
Herr, John, deed to the land of
S1-2 II 361
Herr Family of Manor S4 I 91
Herrington Family AV 1900 28
Herron Family AV 1897 95, 176;
AV 1899 170, 171
Hershereder Family S3 II 208
Hershey Family S3 II 18; S4 I 88;
AV 1896 206
Hess Family AV 1898 174
Heston, Jacob F., of Philadelphia,
note S1-2 II 190
Hetzler Family S3 II 239
Hewitt, Captain Dethick S4 I 140
Hewitt Family S4 I 140
Heydt Family AV 1898 240
Heylman Family AV 1898 241
Hickok, John Hoyt S1-2 I 343
Hiddleson Family S4 II 257
Hiester, Augustus O. S4 II 289
Highspire and its postmasters S3
II 496

Hill (Sand) Church, Parthemore
records S3 I 84; S4 I 34, 43, 46,
48, 49, 52, 54, 59, 61, 63
Hill Church, Berks County records
of AV 1898 169, 173, 178
Hill Church, Lebanon County, rec-
ords of AV 1898 231, 240, 248,
256, 261, 266, 270, 276, 279, 285,
289, 296, 301
Hill Family S3 I 153; AV 1898 190
Hills, Stephen S3 III 150
Himmelberger Family AV 1899
191
Hinckel Family AV 1899 191
Historians, topics for S3 II 286
Historical scraps S3 I 514; S3 II
76, 489; S4 II 8, 23, 44, 53, 68,
188; AV 1898 123; AV 1900 133,
162, 172
Hite Family S4 I 47
Hix Family AV 1898 241
Hoagland Family S4 II 274
Hobson Family AV 1898 190
Hoff Family S4 II 251
Hoffer, Jacob Reider S4 I 101
Hoffman Family S3 I 1
Hoffman Family of Lykens Valley
S1-2 I 211; S3 II 78, 283
Hoffman's Church, Lykens Valley
S4 II 227
Hoffman's Creek S1-2 I 202
Hoffmeister Family AV 1897 165
Hoge, David AV 1896 193
Hoge, James S1-2 II 329
Hoge, Lieutenant John, of the Revo-
lution, letter of S1-2 II 330
Hoge Family, inquiry concerning
AV 1899 215
Hoge Family of Hogestown S1-2 I
471; S1-2 II 72; S3 II 265
Holderbaum Family AV 1897 6;
AV 1898 240
Holgate Family S4 I 139
Holland, Luke, story of S3 II 190

Holland Family, inquiry concern-
ing AV 1897 219
Holliday, Adam, note AV 1897 209
Holliday Family S3 II 201; AV
1896 170; AV 1900 6, 22
Hollinger Family S3 II 275; S4 I
158; S4 II 356; AV 1898 241
Holme, Thomas AV 1899 83
Holme Family AV 1899 148
Holtz Family AV 1898 241
Holtzinger Family AV 1898 190
Home-Missionary episode AV
1896 154
Homstead, historic S4 I 155
Hoover Family S3 I 258; S3 III 402
Hopson, John AV 1896 38
Hopson Family AV 1898 47
Hornberger Family AV 1898 240
Horneilin Family S4 I 246
Horse contracts in 1780 S4 I 44
Horsfield, Timothy S3 III 166
Horter, George Reis S1-2 II 400
Horter Family S1-2 I 347, 357; AV
1896 87
"Hotch-Potch, The" S3 I 191
Hottenstein Family AV 1899 219
House Family S3 II 441
Houser Family S3 II 276; S4 I 113
Houston, Dr. John AV 1897 18
Houston Family S4 I 69; AV 1896
128, 146
Howard Family S3 II 121
Howe, Lord, and Dr. Franklin AV
1900 196
Howe, Sir William, report of, 1777
AV 1897 160
Hoyer, George AV 1900 79
Huber Family AV 1898 240, 241
Huber Family grave-yard S3 I 108
Hubley, Captain Bernard AV 1897
13
Hubley Family AV 1896 183; AV
1897 200, 204; AV 1898 1
Hucks, Christian, note AV 1897 175

Hudson Family S3 III 514
"Hue and Cry" in 1707 S3 III 515
Huffnagle, Peter S1-2 I 485
Huffnagle Family S3 II 243
Huguenot settlement in Dauphin
County S1-2 I 202
Huguenots of Lykens Valley S3 III
305
Huling Family S3 II 160
Hulings, David Watts, note S1-2 II
191
Hulings, Marcus, family of S1-2
II 192, 210, 424
Hulings Family S1-2 II 88, 114;
AV 1900 35
Hume Family S3 I 153; AV 1900
206
Hummel, Frederick S1-2 I 334
Hummel, Frederick, will of AV
1896 31
Hummelstown Cave S1-2 II 388
Hummelstown in 1771 and 1779
S1-2 I 398
Hummelstown Lutheran Grave-
yard, tombstone records S3 I 9,
13, 19, 24
Hower Family S3 II 143
Humrickhouse Family AV 1898 79;
AV 1900 126
"Hundertjahrige Calender, Der"
S1-2 II 182
Hunter, Colonel Samuel AV 1897
14
Hunter, Thomas, of York County
S1-2 II 329
Hunter Family S3 II 12, 216; S4 II
122; AV 1899 14; AV 1900 223
Hunter Family of Hunter's Fort
S3 II 494
Huntington Friends' Meeting,
tombstone records AV 1897 177
Huppman Family AV 1898 240
Hursh's grave-yard AV 1896 119
Huston Family S3 II 264; S4 I 1;

AV 1900 166
Hutchinson, Thomas S3 III 131
Hutchinson Family S3 I 154; S3 II
264, 276
Hutchison, Joseph S1-2 I 52
Hutchison Family S4 I 41, 63; AV
1900 195

I

Illinois and Wabash, United Com-
panies of AV 1897 85
Imboden Family AV 1896 14; AV
1898 241, 242
Immigration into New York from
Pennsylvania S1-2 I 312
Inauguration, first S3 III 524
"Indian burying ground", inquiry
concerning S1-2 II 364
Indian captives of Boquet's expe-
dition S1-2 I 132
Indian family record S3 I 86, 118
Indian geographical names S1-2 I
99, 109, 353
Indian graves, glass beads in AV
1898 269
Indian hominy stone AV 1898 65
Indian implements S3 I 250
Indian letter S3 III 487
Indian marauding in 1794 S4 I 90
Indian mound on Clemson's Island
S4 I 48
Indian names S1-2 II 46; AV 1897 9
Indian names (Iroquois) S3 III 63,
162
Indian names, Heckewelder on S3
III 238, 244, 251, 254
Indian names given to missionar-
ies S3 II 149
Indian names in western Pennsyl-
vania S4 I 21, 71
Indian names of trees, shrubs, etc.
S3 II 401
Indian genealogy S3 II 490

Indian outrages in Cumberland
County S3 II 423
Indian purchase, old S1-2 II 458
Indian Town, the S1-2 I 14, 152
Indian traders, Biscay axes of
S1-2 II 208
Indian traders, recusant, in 1749
S1-2 I 403
Indian trails AV 1898 42
Indian tribes, Nanticokes and
Shawanese S3 I 303
Indian tribes in 1764 S3 III 319
Indian words (Shawanese) S3 III
364
Indiana, history of AV 1899 224
Indians, bad, in 1776 S3 II 275
Indians, Purchases from, prior to
the coming of Penn S3 II 75
Indians at Wekquitank in 1760 AV
1899 125
Indians noted in Pennsylvania his-
tory S1-2 II 436, 460
Ingram, Samuel D. S4 II 95
Innis, Brice S1-2 II 215
Innis Family S3 I 518; S4 I 120
Inns, note S3 I 271
Ireland Family S3 II 277
Irish, Elizabeth Thomas AV 1899
72
Iroquois league S3 I 279
Iron masters, old letters from S3
II 256
Iroquois Indian names S3 III 63,
162
Irvine, Sarah Harris S4 I 308
Irvine Family S3 II 186; AV 1896
125
Irwin, Dr. James S4 I 118
Irwin, Colonel Jared AV 1897 122
Irwin, Jean McDowell S4 I 325
Irwin, John AV 1898 172
Irwin, Matthew AV 1898 172
Irwin Family S3 II 341; S4 I 286;
S4 II 97, 345; AV 1897 122; AV

1898 190; AV 1899 117
Isenhour, Casper S1-2 I 139

J

Jack, Matthew, a hero of the Revolution AV 1896 175
Jack, Captain Patrick S1-2 II 305; S4 I 118
Jack Family AV 1896 54, 138
Jackson, President Andrew, inquiry concerning bust of S1-2 II 197
Jackson Family AV 1899 149
Jameson, Jacob S1-2 I 377
Jamison Family S3 II 277; S4 I 91
Jaquette, Peter, death of AV 1896 159
Javin Family AV 1897 40
Jefferson, Joseph, the elder S1-2 I 335
Jefferson County in 1820 S4 I 45
Jefferson Family S3 II 148
Jenkins, Steuben S3 III 506
Jenkins Family AV 1899 215
Jennings Family AV 1899 91
Jensel Family AV 1898 242
Jews, at Lancaster, in 1744 S3 I 291
Job Family S3 II 127
Johns Family S3 II 246
Johnson, Mrs. Jane A. S4 I 66
Johnson, Ovid Frazer S1-2 I 335
Johnson Family S3 II 456; S4 II 173, 307; AV 1896 180; AV 1897 144; AV 1898 242
Johnston, James S4 I 118
Johnston, Martha Beatty S4 I 327
Johnston, Dr. Robert S4 I 118
Johnston Family S3 II 127, 277; S3 III 165; AV 1899 170; AV 1900 156
Johnston Family of Antrim S1-2 I 449
Johnstown, Pennsylvania, inquiry

concerning AV 1897 230
Jones, Uriah James S1-2 II 215
Jones Family S3 II 79; S4 II 71; AV 1899 149, 158
Joppa (Maryland), on Gunpowder River S3 I 273
Jordan, Benjamin S3 III 559
Jordan, Colonel Francis AV 1900 84
Jordan Family S3 III 130; S4 I 74; S4 II 247
Jordan Lutheran Church, Lehigh County, tombstone records AV 1899 45
Jotter Family AV 1898 241
"Jumping the Bullie" S1-2 I 25
Jungblutt Family AV 1898 242
Jungmann Family S3 II 237
Juniata in 1789 S3 II 350
Juniata Island, Brainard's visit to, in 1745 S1-2 I 274
Jury, Abraham S1-2 I 205
Jury Family S4 I 112
Justices, early S3 I 12; S4 I 54

K

Kachlein Family AV 1900 52
Kahnweiler, Joseph AV 1900 109
Kaltglesser Family AV 1899 102
Kamerer Family S1-2 II 397
Kapp, Amos, reminiscences of S3 II 360
Kapp Family S4 I 113
Karmenie Family AV 1898 244, 245
Keagle Family, inquiry concerning S3 III 216
Keagy, Dr. John M. S1-2 I 247, 335
Keagy Family S3 II 278
Kean, General John S1-2 I 408; S1-2 II 450; S3 III 90, 93, 100, 106, 111
Kean Family S3 III 114

Kearsley Family AV 1900 1, 5
Keblinger Family AV 1899 191
Keck Family AV 1899 224
Keefer, Reverend D. W. S4 I 87
Keeley Family AV 1897 181, 191
Keen Family AV 1899 152
Keene, Major Lawrence AV 1897 131
Keiler Family S3 II 216
Keim, General George M. AV 1898 143
Keim Family AV 1898 121, 143
Keimer Family S3 III 46; AV 1897 204, 227
Keiser Family AV 1899 43
Kelker, Anthony S1-2 I 336
Kelker, Mrs. Henry A. S4 I 181
Kelker, John S1-2 II 220
Kell, James, of York AV 1899 86
Keller, John Peter S1-2 II 401
Keller, Simon S4 I 105
Keller Family AV 1897 125; AV 1898 243; AV 1899 191
Kelly Family of Londonderry S3 II 84; S3 III 63; AV 1896 198
Kelso, William S1-2 II 450
Kelso Family S1-2 II 113; S4 I 108; AV 1899 86
Kemble, Dr. George S. S3 III 411
Kendell Family AV 1899 209
Kendig, Martin S1-2 II 220, 360
Kennedy, Robert S1-2 II 221
Kennedy Family S3 I 221; S3 II 216; AV 1896 233; AV 1899 160
Kercher Family AV 1899 191
Kerlin, John, of Chester, note S1-2 II 189
Kern, Lieutenant Jacob, journal of, in 1758 S3 II 124
Kern Family AV 1899 191; AV 1900 72
Kerr, Reverend William S1-2 II 401
Kerr, Reverend William, call to S1-2 I 58

Kerr Family S3 I 175
Kesler, George P. S4 I 107
Kessinger Family S3 III 174
Keyler Family AV 1897 96
Kichel Family AV 1899 191
Kiefer Family S3 II 232
Kiester Family AV 1899 225
Kilgore Family S3 II 159; AV 1899 109
Killinger Family S3 II 238
Kilmer Family S4 II 276
Kimmering Family AV 1898 245
King, Robert, note S4 I 172, 179
King Family S3 I 22; S4 I 119, 179; AV 1898 231
Kingsford, Mrs., school of S1-2 I 10, 105
Kinkead Family AV 1899 160
Kinneard, John D. AV 1897 119
Kinnersley Family AV 1899 153
Kintzer Family AV 1898 245
Kirber Family AV 1898 244
Kirby, William C. AV 1896 137
Kirkbride Family AV 1896 60, 72
Kirkpatrick, Ann AV 1899 60
Kirkpatrick Family AV 1899 32
Kirkpatrick farm S3 I 509
Kirkwood Family S3 I 175
Kisner Family S3 II 207, 210
Kissner Family AV 1898 242
"Kitohtening Mills" or Fort Hunter S1-2 I 415
Kittanning, expenses of the survey at S1-2 II 268
Kittera, John Wilkes S1-2 I 484
Kittera Family S3 II 166; S4 I 277; AV 1898 86
KittnerFamily AV 1899 191
Kittring Family AV 1898 242
Kitzmiller Family AV 1900 198
Kitzsch Family S3 II 192
Kleber Family AV 1898 245
Klee Family AV 1899 192
Kleeman Family AV 1898 243

Klein Family AV 1898 174, 245
Klinger Family AV 1899 53
Kloppen Church S1-2 I 357; AV 1896 114
Kneisly Family S4 I 97
Knight Family AV 1900 16, 59
Knoll Family AV 1899 192
Knopff Family AV 1899 192
Knox Family S3 II 238
Knupp Family S3 I 175
Kob Family AV 1898 244
Kober Family AV 1898 242, 244
Koch Family S3 II 78
Kochendoerffer Family AV 1899 192
Koehl Family AV 1899 192
Kohl Family AV 1898 46
Kolmar Family AV 1898 244
Konigmacher Family AV 1899 175
Koontz Family S3 II 278
Koppenheffer, Simon, note S1-2 II 390
Koppenheffer Family AV 1900 195
Kraemer Family S3 II 221, 244, 245
Krafft Family AV 1899 192
Kramer Family S3 II 176
Krause, David, Jr. S1-2 II 221
Krause, David, Sr. S1-2 II 221
Kreider, Mrs. Susan S4 I 94
Kreider Family S4 I 113; AV 1900 53
Krone Family S4 I 120
Krueger Family AV 1898 243, 244
Kucher Family AV 1898 242, 244
Kueffer Family AV 1898 242, 245
Kuehler Family AV 1899 192
Kunkel, Christian S1-2 II 222
Kunkel Family AV 1896 32
Kuntz Family AV 1898 174
Kupper Family S3 II 127
Kurtz Family S3 III 513
Kyle, James S1-2 I 322

L

Labar, Daniel S4 I 107
Lacey, General John, memoranda from papers AV 1900 134
Lafayette in Harrisburg S3 II 493
Laird, Samuel S1-2 I 358; S1-2 II 450
Laird Family S3 I 176; S3 II 468; S4 I 138; AV 1896 218
Lamb Family S3 II 294
Lancaster, British prisoners at S1-2 II 354, 380
Lancaster, Lafayette's visit to S4 II 209
Lancaster, Moravian Church, pastors of S3 III 417
Lancaster, old courthouse at S3 I 277
Lancaster, Reformed Church records AV 1900 158
Lancaster, St. James Church, baptisms AV 1900 202, 206, 214
Lancaster, St. James Church, marriage records AV 1897 3, 11, 16, 19, 25, 27, 37, 42, 51
Lancaster, St. Mary's Church, baptisms AV 1900 124
Lancaster, St. Mary's Church, list of clergy S4 II 108
Lancaster baptisms, early AV 1900 124
Lancaster barracks S4 II 280, 285, 291, 300
Lancaster County burials, 1841-1856 AV 1899 178
Lancaster, St. Mary's Church AV 1896 131
Lancaster County divorces, 1788-1800 AV 1899 101
Lancaster County flying camp, orderly book AV 1900 10
Lancaster County marriage licen-

ses 1791-1799 S3 II 297, 304, 311, 316
Lancaster County historical society AV 1896 153
Lancaster Court cases S1-2 I 446
Lancaster orphans court records AV 1900 194
Lancaster Phalanx in the War of 1812 AV 1900 5
Land warrants S3 III 135, 140, 151, 154
Landes Family AV 1899 175
Landis, John S1-2 II 463, 464, 469; AV 1899 122, 143
Landis, Samuel S1-2 II 223
Landis Family S3 I 16; S3 III 34; S4 I 13
Lane Family S3 I 26
Lang (Long) Family S3 II 451; AV 1898 245; AV 1899 192
Lange Family S3 II 209
Lanius Family S4 II 245, 246, 250
Lantz Family S3 III 434
Larch Family S4 I 114
LaRue Family S3 III 123; S4 I 120
Latcha Family AV 1900 58
Lathey, Dr. William Kent S4 I 117
Latin, political poem in, of 1800 S1-2 I 218
Latta Family S4 I 62
Lauer Family AV 1898 171, 245
Lauman, William S1-2 I 359
"Laurel Hill", inquiry concerning S1-2 I 177, 196
Laverty, Jesse S4 I 67
Law suit, an old S3 II 412
Lawlor Family S3 II 294
Lawrence, George V., note S4 II 222
Lawrence, Captain John, note AV 1897 65
Lawson, David, of Armstrong, note S1-2 II 190
Lawson's Island S3 I 1; AV 1896 197
Leacock Presbyterian Church, tombstone records AV 1897 79
Leavitt Family AV 1899 109
Lebanon, First Reformed Church, baptisms AV 1900 88
Lebo Family AV 1900 35
Lecron Family S3 II 127
Leddick, Philip AV 1899 5
Ledis Family S3 II 294
Lee, Captain Andrew, of Paxtang S1-2 I 167, 223, 229; S1-2 II 271 AV 1896 109
Lee, Washington, recommendation AV 1896 110
Lee Family S3 I 83
Leech, George, inquiry concerning S1-2 II 263
Leech, Richard Treat S4 I 314
Leech Family S3 III 557
Lefler Family AV 1899 44
Legislative anecdote S3 III 404
Legislative sketches half a century ago S1-2 II 186
Legislators of 1813-1814 S1-2 I 292, 304
Legislature of 1828-1829 S3 III 141
Lehigh River, early fishing on the S3 II 261; S3 III 213
Lehman, William, of Philadelphia S1-2 II 189, 271
Lehman Family S3 II 128
Lehn Family AV 1898 46
Leonhard Family S4 II 37; AV 1899 193
Lerch Family AV 1899 192
Leroy Family (LeRoy) S3 III 507
LeRoy Family AV 1900 223
Lesher Family AV 1900 68
Letter carriers, first, at Harrisburg S1-2 II 134, 147
Letter of the old time AV 1899 117

Lewis, Major Eli S1-2 I 359
Lewis, (David), reminiscences of
the robber S1-2 I 446; S3 I 337
Lewis Co. AV 1899 163
Lewis Family AV 1896 60; AV
1899 153
Lieb Family AV 1899 214
Lincoln, Abraham, ancestry of
S3 III 479
Lincoln, Abraham, renomination
of S3 I 40
Lind, Reverend Matthew S1-2 I 19
Lindley Family S3 I 25
Lingle Family S4 I 113; AV 1899
192, 193, 214
Linn, John Blair AV 1898 294
Linn, Reverend William S1-2 I
466
Linn Family S4 I 90; AV 1899 68
Lisburn, Yellow Fever at, in 1803
S1-2 II 296
Lisson Family S4 II 115
Lititz, tombstone records AV
1896 87
Litle Family AV 1900 191
Little Family S4 II 341
Litz Family AV 1898 245
Livinghouse Family AV 1899 61
Lloyd Family AV 1899 158
Local history, scraps of S1-2 I
418; S4 I 5
Localities, old inquiry concerning
S3 I 12
Location of national capital S1-2 I
159
Lochman, Reverend George E.
AV 1900 22, 29
Lochman, Reverend John S1-2 II
223
Lochry, Colonel Archibald AV
1899 62
Lochry Family AV 1899 62
Lockart Family AV 1898 66
Lodge, Benjamin, Jr. AV 1896

219
Loeser Family AV 1900 194
Log store AV 1900 136
Logan, James, note to the proprie-
tor S3 II 342
Logan, John, of Londonderry S1-2
II 263
Logan Family S3 I 8; S3 II 217;
S3 III 472; AV 1899 139; AV
1900 209
Lombardy poplars S1-2 I 441
Londonderry (Ireland), the sword
of S1-2 I 256
Londonderry, N. H. S1-2 I 250
Londonderry (Pennsylvania),
assessment in, 1778 S1-2 II 55
Londonderry (Pennsylvania), in
1775 S1-2 I 22
Londonderry (Pennsylvania), Lan-
caster County, in 1777 S3 I 466
Londonderry Township lines S1-2
II 136
Londonderry Township tombstone
records S3 III 57
Londonderry's overseers S4 I 146,
157
Long, Christian S4 I 70
"Long bullets" S1-2 I 5, 25
"Long bullets", Parson Elder on
S1-2 II 197
Long Family S4 I 258; AV 1896
159; AV 1900 173
Lotteries, Church S3 I 425; S4 I
121
Loudon Family S3 II 202
Louisbourg, name of Harrisburg
in 1789 S1-2 II 389
Louisburgh S1-2 I 418
Louther Manor, Paxtang or S3 II
109, 113
Lovett Family AV 1900 145
Lowrey, Ann West (Alricks) S4 I
249
Lowrey Family S4 I 151

Lowry Family S3 I 16
Lubold Family AV 1900 28
Lucas Family S4 II 147
Ludington, James S1-2 II 119
Lukens, Asahel, escape of
S1-2 I 316
Lukens, Jesse, diary of, in 1774
AV 1900 136, 142, 148, 154
Lusk, William AV 1898 172
Lusk Family S3 I 176
Luther, Dr. John S1-2 I 269, 272
Luther Family S3 II 217
Lutz Family AV 1899 193; AV
1900 59
Luzerne, loss of the S3 II 384
Lycans, Andrew S1-2 I 264
Lycans Family S3 I 191
Lycoming County, bibliography of
AV 1897 29
Lycoming County, first taxables
of Muncy Township S4 I 131
Lykens, Zion's Lutheran Church
S4 I 85
Lykens Valley, coal development
S3 II 12
Lykens Valley, St. John's Luther-
an Church, tombstone records
S4 II 167
Lyle Family AV 1898 300
Lytle Family S1-2 I 437; S3 II 216,
278, 429; S3 III 474; S4 I 34, 41
Lytle's Ferry S1-2 I 217

M

McAlarney, Joseph C. AV 1896
143
McAlarney, Mathias Wilson AV
1900 186
McAlister, Sarah Nelson S4 I 291
McAlister Family S3 II 295; AV
1898 176
McAllister Family S3 III 7, 505,
518; S4 I 106; AV 1899 5

McArthur, Duncan AV 1899 237
McArthur Family S3 II 469
MacBeth, Andrew AV 1898 172
MacBeth, Reverend John, note S1-2
II 235, 242
MacBeth Family S3 III 182, 201
McBryar Family AV 1899 63
McCall Family S3 I 177; S3 III
494; AV 1900 9, 145
McCalla Family AV 1897 204, 220
McCallen, Captain Robert, company
of, in the Revolution S1-2 II 200
McCallen Family S3 I 177; AV
1899 181
McCallister, Reverend Richard
S3 II 32
McCallister Family AV 1898 135
McCall's Ferry Bridge, letter
from Theodore Burr on S1-2 II
142
McCalmont Family AV 1897 9
McCamant, James S3 III 357
McCamant Family AV 1900 47
McCammant Family AV 1900 194
McCammon, James S1-2 I 359
McCammon, John S1-2 I 94
McCammon Family S3 I 177
McCann, Patt S3 I 60
McCann Family S3 II 64
McCauley Family AV 1899 154
McClane Family AV 1896 141
McClean, Sarah Holmes AV 1896
209
McClean, William S4 I 317
McClean Family AV 1896 94; AV
1897 223
McClellan, Captain John, company
of, in the Revolution AV 1896
204
McClelland Family AV 1896 161;
AV 1897 8
McClenahan Family S3 II 322
McClung, Matthew, note S1-2 II
315

McClure, David S3 III 413
McClure Family S1-2 II 410; S3 II
79, 134, 214, 487; S4 I 89, 136;
AV 1898 73, 85, 102, 119, 211;
AV 1899 72, 139
McClure Family of Donegal S3 I
491, 498
McConnell, Squire, inquiry con-
cerning S1-2 II 309
McConnell Family S3 I 178; S3 III
502; AV 1900 9
McCord Family S3 I 11; S3 II 276;
S4 I 113
McCorkle Family S3 I 78
McCormick, Martha Sanderson
S4 I 287
McCormick, Colonel Henry AV
1900 98
McCormick Family S3 I 11, 178,
518
McCosh, John S1-2 I 267
McCoy, Robert S3 III 208
McCullough Family S3 II 134; S3
III 508
McCune Family AV 1899 170; AV
1900 10, 69
McCurdy Family AV 1899 232
McDaniel Family S3 II 12; AV
1896 65
McDonald Family AV 1899 14
McDowell Family S4 II 206; AV
1899 107, 189
McElderry Family S4 II 317
McElrath Family S3 I 400; S3 III
174
McFarland, Margaret Lewis S4 I
327
McFarland, Margaret Lynn S4 I
19
McFarland Family S3 I 216; S3 II
119, 121, 137
MacFarlane, Edward, inquiry con-
cerning S1-2 I 353
McGeehon, Duncan S4 I 197

McGowan Family S3 II 321
McIlhenny, Samuel AV 1899 228
McIlhenny Family AV 1900 195
McIlvaine Family S4 I 102
McJimsey, Joseph A. S4 I 314
Mack, Reverend John Martin,
journal of a visit to the Onon-
dagoes S3 II 50, 58, 64
McKean, Samuel S3 III 195
McKean, Governor Thomas, ad-
ministration of AV 1897 93
McKean, Governor Thomas, letter
of S1-2 II 281
McKee, Martha Hoge S4 II 5
McKee, Robert S3 I 216; S3 III 92
McKee, Captain Robert, militia
company of, in 1783-88 S3 I
471
McKee, Thomas, Indian trader
S1-2 II 265
McKeehan Family AV 1900 9
McKennan, Captain William S4 I
275
McKinley Family AV 1898 176
McKinney, Mordecai S1-2 II 402;
S4 I 318
McKinney Family S3 II 295, 324;
AV 1900 9
McKnight, John S4 I 1
McKnight Family S3 II 296; AV
1897 124; AV 1899 171
Maclay, Andrew, inquiry concern-
ing S3 I 3
Maclay, Dr. Samuel S4 I 78
Maclay Family AV 1899 170
Maclean, Moses, of Dauphin, note
S1-2 II 191
McLean Family S4 I 304
McLene Family AV 1899 112
McMeans Family S4 II 158, 298
McMillan, Reverend John, visits
to churches of AV 1900 65
McMordie Family AV 1900 126
McNair, Governor Alexander, of

Missouri S1-2 II 429
McNair Family AV 1899 101
McNeely Family S1-2 II 216; S3 I 217
McNees Family AV 1896 245
McNeill Family of Montgomery County S4 I 159
McNutt (McKnight) Family S3 II 294
McPherson, Agnes Miller AV 1898 295
McPherson, Margaret Stout AV 1898 131
McPherson Family AV 1896 94; AV 1898 59
McQueen Family S3 II 134; S3 III 1; S4 I 103
McQuown, Captain Richard, company of, in the Revolution S1-2 II 45
McQuown Family S3 I 217
McRoberts Family S4 I 65, 113
McVaugh Family AV 1899 153
Magaw, Marritie Van Brunt S4 I 283
Magaw, Colonel Robert S1-2 I 468
Magaw Family S4 I 125
Maghee Family AV 1899 153
Maginness, James, reminiscences of S1-2 II 1
Maginnis, James S1-2 I 360
Magnetic telegraph office at Harrisburg S1-2 I 252, 257
Magraw, James, letter of, in 1733 S1-2 II 3
Magraw, Reverend S3 I 201
Maharg Family AV 1896 219
Maher, Reverend Pierce S1-2 I 360
Mahon Family AV 1897 95; AV 1899 170
Makemie Family S4 I 149, 301; AV 1897 126
"Manaday Township" S3 I 221

Manners and customs S3 I 4, 26; S3 III 327
Manning, Captain Richard, company of S1-2 I 425
Marbourg Family AV 1900 136
Marcker Family AV 1898 245
Marietta volunteer militia S4 II 8
Maris Family AV 1899 153
Markley, Dr. George H. AV 1900 80
Marks, William S3 III 48
Marple Family AV 1899 153
Marquis Family AV 1900 42, 43
Marr Family AV 1897 59
Marriages, early S3 I 510, 516, 524; AV 1900 122
Marriages by the Reverend DeWit S3 II 473
Marsh Creek, early settlers on AV 1896 139
Marsh Creek Presbyterian Churc AV 1898 8
Marshall, Captain John, company of, in the Revolution S1-2 II 1;
Marshall Family S3 II 295; AV 1897 178; AV 1898 17; AV 1899 53, 151; AV 1900 75
Marshe's journal of the Lancaste Treaty S3 I 264-305
Marsteller Family S4 I 1
Martin, Reverend James, neglect grave of AV 1898 168
Martin, Robert, first settler at Northumberland Point AV 189 234
Martin, Reverend Samuel A., memorial sermon at Derry S3 I 316
Martin Family AV 1896 130; AV 1898 245; AV 1899 175; AV 190 174
Martin Family of Northumberlan S3 I 218; S3 III 242; S4 I 51; A 1896 235

Martinsburg (Virginia) S1-2 I 489
Mason and Dixon line S3 III 193
Masonic funerals, early S3 II 105; AV 1899 162
Masonic pitcher S1-2 I 89
Masser Family AV 1897 190
Matter Family S3 II 80; AV 1898 247
Matter Family, inquiry concerning S3 I 22
Matthews, George S4 I 1
Matthews Family AV 1899 108
Mau Family AV 1898 247
Mauck Family AV 1898 175
Maurer Family AV 1896 246
Maus Family AV 1897 132
Mause, Philip AV 1896 203
Maxwell, Captain James S4 I 205
Maxwell, Major William S4 I 205
Maxwell Family S3 II 128
Maybane Family S3 I 372
Mayer, Benjamin S3 III 113
Mayer Family AV 1898 129, 175
Mayes Family S3 I 219
Mays Family S3 II 121
Mead Family S4 II 123
Means, Damuel S1-2 I 224
Means Family S3 I 220; S4 II 86; AV 1897 42; AV 1898 239; AV 1899 209
Mears, Captain John S4 I 257
Meason, Isaac AV 1897 68
Mechanics, young tramping S4 I 156
Meckley, Susanna Miller S4 I 326
Meese Family S3 II 143
Meetch, John S1-2 II 403
Meeth Family AV 1899 193
Meeting-House Springs, records of S3 II 478; S4 I 190, 193
Meginness, John Franklin AV 1899 172, 180, 195; AV 1900 131
Meharg Family AV 1899 68
Melish, John S1-2 I 361

Melsheimer Family AV 1898 246
Memorial Day, origin of AV 1898 125
Meng Family, inquiry concerning S4 I 117
Mennonite Church, oldest in Dauphin County AV 1896 60
Mentzer Family AV 1898 246; AV 1899 33
Mercer, Mrs. Isabella, note AV 1899 224
Mercer, Colonel James, family of S1-2 II 365
Mercer Family S4 I 63; AV 1899 201
Meredith and Clymer Estate AV 1896 175
"Mertz" Church, Rockland Township, Berks County, early records of AV 1900 66, 70, 75, 81
Mervine Family AV 1898 230
Messerschmidt Family AV 1899 193
"Methiglia" S4 I 161
Methodism in 1796 S3 I 200
Metz, Sarah Fisher AV 1899 233
Metz Family AV 1899 233
Mexican War, Pennsylvania in the S3 III 499
Mexico's Capital, first old glory at AV 1896 76
Meyer Family S3 II 231; S4 II 246; AV 1899 193
Meyle Family AV 1898 245
Meylert, Secku AV 1896 193
Meylert Family AV 1896 196
Meyrick Family S3 II 73
Michael Family AV 1899 193
Middle Octorara Church AV 1897 143
Middle Ridge Church graveyard S4 I 267
Middle Spring Presbyterian Church AV 1900 65

Middle Spring Presbyterian
   Church tombstone records AV
   1899 169
Middleton Family S3 I 220
Middletown, graveyard at S1-2 II
   376, 390
Middletown, notes concerning
   S1-2 II 391; S3 III 247
Middletown, St. Peter's Lutheran
   Church S3 I 235; S4 I 8, 9, 13
Middletown, St. Peter's Lutheran
   Church tombstone records S3 I
   222, 233; S3 I 528
Middletown assessment in 1775
   S1-2 II 15
Middletown assessment in 1789
   S1-2 II 385
"Middletown-on-the-Swatara"
   S1-2 II 378
Middletown patriotism S3 II 8
Middletown Presbyterian grave-
   yard tombstone records S3 III
   34; S4 II 80
Middletown United Brethren Church
   tombstone records S3 II 41
Mifflin, Thomas S3 III 530
Mifflin, Governor Thomas, inau-
   guration of S3 III 524
Mifflinburg tombstone records
   AV 1899 89
Milchsach Family AV 1898 47
Miles Family AV 1898 146; AV
   1899 153
Military company in Hanover S3
   III 75
Military spirit in 1786 S1-2 I 303
Military spirit in 1821 S1-2 I 302
Militia company in 1823 S4 I 7
Militia officers in 1806 and 1807
   S3 II 459
Militia of the Revolution S3 II 41
Militia roll S3 I 5, 12; S4 II 87
Militia roll of 1839 AV 1900 116
Mill on the Swatara S3 I 3

Miller, Colonel Henry S1-2 I 146
Miller, Jacob, deed to the land of
   S1-2 II 362
Miller, Robert AV 1898 172
Miller Family S3 I 16, 533; S3 II
   73, 134; S3 III 149, 406; S4 I 1,
   95, 100, 141, 159; AV 1898 145,
   175; AV 1899 20, 193; AV 1900
   9, 69
Miller Family of York County AV
   1897 132
Millerite delusion of 1843 S4 I 68
Millersburg, founding of S1-2 I
   262
Millerstown on the Juniata S4 I 4
Mills, old S1-2 I 439; S3 II 489
Milroy Family S3 I 239; AV 1898
   248
Milton (Pennsylvania), founder of
   AV 1897 41
Milton (Pennsylvania), tombstone
   records S4 I 120
Milton Grove Cemetery, tomb-
   stone records AV 1897 46
Minnick Family S3 I 239
Minshall Family S3 II 166; S3 III
   510
Minsker, Ludwig, of Clark's Val-
   ley S1-2 I 410, 436
Minsker Family S3 I 221
Misner Family AV 1899 226
Mitchell, Alexander, deposition of
   S1-2 II 167, 181; S3 I 236
Mitchell, Andrew S1-2 II 224
Mitchell, General David S3 III 47
Mitchell Family S3 I 240; S4 I 97;
   AV 1898 87; AV 1899 49; AV
   1900 9, 168, 192
Molyneux Family S4 II 150, 339
Monaghan Presbyterian Church,
   tombstone records AV 1897
   164
Monroe County AV 1896 132
Monteith, Captain James, inquiry

concerning S1-2 I 1
Montfort Family AV 1897 104
Montgomery, Daniel AV 1897 104
Montgomery, John S3 III 48
Montgomery, Reverend Joseph,
  notes S1-2 I 152; S4 I 35
Montgomery, Rachel S1-2 I 361
Montgomery, Robert, letter from
  S3 I 535
Montgomery, William S3 III 413
Montgomery Family S3 I 78; S3 II
  296, 322; S3 III 41, 311, 565; S4
  I 216; AV 1897 97, 104; AV 1899
  215 .
Montour, Madame S3 III 204
Montour Family S3 I 118, 293; S3
  II 236; S4 II 327
Moore, William S4 I 1
Moore Family S3 II 321, 455; S4 I
  102; AV 1896 219; AV 1899 153
Moore Family of Donegal and
  Hempfield S3 II 455
Moorehead, Elizabeth Thompson
  AV 1896 103
Moorehead, Isaac, of Erie S1-2 II
  154
Moorehead, General James K. S3
  III 411
Moorehead Family S3 I 4; S4 I 62
Moravian Congregation in Phila-
  delphia in 1766 AV 1896 212
Moravian emigrants S4 I 162, 167,
  169, 174, 208, 303
Moravian Families AV 1898 45
Moravian ordinations, 1742-92
  S4 I 79
Moravian records at Lebanon S3
  II 354
Moravian records in York County
  S4 II 245, 250, 254
Moravian settlement in Bethel
  Township AV 1897 70
Moravians AV 1900 141
Moravians, register of, 1747-1799

S4 II 1
Morel Family S3 I 476
Morgan, William, note S1-2 II 417
Morgan Family AV 1897 226; AV
  1898 247
Morris Family AV 1899 201
Morrison, Reverend Hugh AV
  1897 120
Morrison, Captain James, com-
  pany of AV 1900 166
Morrison Family S3 III 278
Morrow, Jeremiah, Governor of
  Ohio S4 I 285
Morton, John AV 1899 91
Morus Multicaulis craze, 1836-41
  AV 1899 197
Moser Family AV 1898 174
Motter Family AV 1896 220; AV
  1897 169
Motz Family AV 1899 166
Mournful tragedy of James Bird
  (poem) S1-2 I 260
Mowry, Charles S1-2 II 403
Moyer, Hans, family of S1-2 II
  306
Moyer, Henry, family of S1-2 II
  376
Moyer Family S3 I 240; AV 1898
  135
Mueller Family S3 II 230; AV
  1898 246; AV 1899 193, 194,
  205
Muench, Reverend Charles Ed-
  ward S1-2 I 205
Muench, Daniel A. S4 II 247
Muench Family AV 1899 205
Mumma, Major David S4 I 200
Mumma Family S4 I 95; AV 1897
  117
Murdock Family AV 1900 42
Murdock Family of Conewago
  S1-2 II 42
Murray, Captain James S1-2 I
  425

Murray, Captain James, company of S1-2 I 7
Murray, Colonel John S1-2 I 2, 203, 362
Murray, Dr. Leckey S4 II 242
Murray, Lindley, the grammarian S1-2 I 27, 48, 58, 81
Murray, Margaret Mayes AV 1898 250
Murray Family S1-2 II 365; S3 II 202, 295; S4 II 242
Musgrave, William S4 II 52
Musical recollections S1-2 II 161
Mylin, Martin, deed to the land of S1-2 II 361

N

Nagel, Frederick S4 I 104
Nagle, Colonel George S4 II 46
Nagle, Captain Peter S4 II 47
Nail manufactory S3 II 86
Names, origin of S3 I 193
Nathan, Peter ("Black Pete") S1-2 II 264
Nanticoke Indians S3 I 303
National Capital, location of S1-2 I 159; S3 I 396
Nazareth, Barony of S4 I 98, 101
Nazareth, tombstone records S4 I 111, 114, 115
Neal Family S3 I 241
Naef (Neff) Family AV 1898 247
Neff Family AV 1896 8; AV 1898 247
Negro slavery, days of S3 II 41
Negro slaves belonging to members of Moravian congregation in Philadelphia, in 1766 AV 1896 215
Neidig Family S3 I 507
Neidig's meeting-house S3 II 391
Neilson, John S4 I 314
Nelson Family S3 II 296

Neu (Ney) Family AV 1898 247
Neville, Winifred Oldham AV 1898 213
Neville Family S3 II 358, 369; S3 III 134
Nevin Family AV 1899 171
New Berlin, burials at AV 1898 66
New England Run S3 I 1
New Hanover Lutheran Church at Falkner's Swamp, records of AV 1898 183, 188, 192, 207
New Jersey Loyalists S3 II 406
New York, Pennsylvania immigration into S1-2 I 312
New York, western, early Pennsylvania German settlers in AV 1897 1; AV 1898 90, 99, 110, 120, 140
Newberry (Garretson) meeting-house AV 1900 110
Newspapers, early S3 II 162
Newville (Cumberland County), Big Spring Grave-yard AV 1897 117
Newville (Cumberland County), Big Spring Grave-yard tombstone records AV 1897 147
Newville (Cumberland County), tombstone records nearby AV 1898 206
Newville (Cumberland County), United Presbyterian Graveyard tombstone records AV 1897 127
Newville (Dauphin County) S1-2 I 262
Ney Family AV 1898 247
Nicholas Family AV 1899 158
Nicknames of states S3 II 178
Nieman Family, murder of the AV 1897 145
Nisley Family S3 I 22
Nissley Family S3 II 78
Nivin Family S4 II 297
Nixon Family AV 1899 209

Noland Family S3 II 246
Norris, Captain A. Wilson AV
    1900 1
Northampton County in the Revo-
    lution AV 1900 223
Northampton County wills, early
    AV 1900 52
Northampton County, worthies
    S4 I 122, 135, 137, 177, 180, 183
Northrop Family AV 1899 153
Northumberland, first burgess of
    AV 1899 113
Northumberland County protho-
    notaries AV 1899 226
Northumberland County worthies
    AV 1896 171, 180
Nugent Family S4 I 142
Nye Family S3 II 176, 182, 220, 244

O

Oak Dale Forge S1-2 I 378
Oath of Allegiance in 1777-79
    S1-2 I 227, 231, 236
O'Bannon Family S3 II 358, 369;
    S3 III 134
Oberlander Family S3 II 31
O'Brien Family S3 III 42
O'Caine Family S4 I 142
Oehrle (Early) Family AV 1898
    247; AV 1899 21, 95
Oehrlin Family AV 1899 21, 95
Oehrly Family S3 II 208
Oenslager, John AV 1898 263
Ogden Family, inquiry concerning
    AV 1899 152
Ogiheta, death of AV 1896 159
Ogilby Family S4 II 3, 8
Ogle, Alexander, of Somerset S1-2
    II 189; S3 III 125
Ogle Family S3 III 103
O'Hail Family AV 1897 174
O'Hale Family AV 1899 139
O'Hara, Mary Carson AV 1898 159

O'Hara Family S4 I 289
Ohio, adventures of two French-
    men in the valley of the S3 II
    470
Ohio, settlement of AV 1896 128
Ohl, John S4 I 105
Ohl Family AV 1900 113
Oil, crude, eighty years ago S3 II
    105
Okely Family AV 1898 46
Oley Reformed Church records
    AV 1900 128
O'Neal Family S3 II 322
Opequon, the AV 1899 129
Opickon Church, Virginia S1-2 I
    493
Oppenhauser Family AV 1898 247
Orphan Asylum in Harrisburg
    S1-2 II 423
Orphan's Court of Dauphin County
    S1-2 II 296
Orth, Adam Henry S1-2 II 405
Orth, Rosina Kucker S4 I 292
Orth Family S1-2 I 383
Otsequette, Peter, death of AV
    1896 159
Ott, Leander Nicholas AV 1896 216
Otto Family AV 1900 58

P

Packer, Mrs. Mary Wykoff S4 II
    42
Painted Post, the S4 I 220, 229
Palm Family S3 II 181, 243
Palmstown S1-2 I 234
Palmyra, original name of S1-2
    I 234
Pancake, George S4 II 182
Pannekuchen Family AV 1898 248
Paoli, surprise at AV 1900 92
Paper Mill, an early S4 I 105
Pardoe Family S4 II 311
Paris Family S3 III 278

Park Family S3 I 242
Parke, Benjamin S1-2 II 362
Parke, Margaret AV 1899 9
Parmentere, John, death of S3 I
200
Parthemore, Jacob Shuster AV
1898 291
Partisanship, a case of offensive
S3 II 87
Partridge's Military School at
Harrisburg S1-2 I 61, 72, 84
Party names S3 II 176
Passport, an old AV 1897 160
Past and present contrasted AV
1897 64
Pastorius Family AV 1899 156
Patterson, Galbraith S1-2 II 328
Patterson, Captain James, roll of
company in the French and In-
dian War S3 II 92
Patterson, Mary S1-2 I 355
Patterson, William S1-2 I 346;
S1-2 II 305
Patterson and Potter Families
S1-2 II 304
Patterson and Wirtz Families
S1-2 I 59
Patterson Family S3 I 242, 476;
S3 II 119, 406; S3 III 565; S4 I
61; AV 1899 20, 95, 170
Patton, Samuel S4 I 122
Patton Family S3 I 243; S3 III 512
Pawling Family S4 I 142
Paxtang, or Paxton, meaning of
names S1-2 I 251
Paxtang, North End of, assess-
ment of S1-2 I 95
Paxtang, or Louther Manor S3 II
109, 113
Paxtang, papers relating to S1-2
II 519
Paxtang, petition of inhabitants of
S3 II 228
Paxtang assessment for 1770

S1-2 I 179
Paxtang assessment for 1775 S1-2
II 15
Paxtang assessment for 1789 S1-2
II 385
Paxtang Banditti S3 I 130
Paxtang Boys S1-2 I 2, 107, 434;
S1-2 II 424, 427; S3 I 330; AV
1896 141
Paxtang Church S1-2 I 82, 95; S3 I
44; AV 1900 28, 65
Paxtang Church, admissions, 1807-
42 S1-2 II 135
Paxtang Church, baptismal records
S1-2 I 430; AV 1898 54
Paxtang Church, deaths in 1808
S1-2 I 422
Paxtang Church, dismissions,
1807-42 S1-2 II 178
Paxtang Church, marriage records
S1-2 I 380; AV 1898 54
Paxtang Church, subscriptions to
Mr. Snowden's salary S1-2 II
279
Paxtang Church, tombstone rec-
ords S3 I 409, 414, 423, 428, 435,
438, 508, 520, 536, 543, 556, 558
Paxtang Company before Quebec
in 1775 S3 I 458
Paxtang Covenanter Meeting-house
S1-2 II 468
Paxtang Glebe, deed to S3 III 53
Paxtang in 1756 S3 III 503
Paxtang prices 130 years ago S1-2
II 207
Paxtang Valley, contributions to
southern refugees in 1781 S1-2
II 356
Paxtang Valley, schools and
schoolmasters of S1-2 II 299
Paxtang Valley, weddings in S1-2
II 351, 352
Paxtang Valley, witch craft in
S1-2 II 272

Paxtang volunteers in 1779 S1-2 I 349
Paxton, see Paxtang
Paxton Family AV 1896 43; AV 1898 176
Paxton Family of Marsh Creek S3 III 270, 512; AV 1900 33
Peacock, James S1-2 I 247, 362; S4 I 70, 75
Pearce, Stewart, ancestry of S1-2 II 310
Pearson, Richard, family of S1-2 II 451
Pease Family AV 1900 10
Peebles, Captain Robert S4 I 205
Peebles Family S3 II 203
Peffer Family S3 I 243
Pegram Family S4 II 307
Penn, John, visit to Harrisburg S1-2 I 135
Penn, Governor Thomas, at Harris' Ferry S1-2 II 313
Penn, William, and his province S1-2 II 139
Penn, William, Bi-Centennial celebration of the landing of, in America S1-2 II 417, 451
Penn Family AV 1896 233
Penn landing day S1-2 II 417, 451
Penn portraits S1-2 II 306
Pennepeck Baptist Church, tombstone records AV 1899 147
Pennock Family AV 1899 53
Penn's first surveyor general AV 1899 83
Penn's Valley (Pennsylvania), Heckman's Church AV 1900 195
Pennsylvania, capital of S1-2 II 285
Pennsylvania, first iron works in S3 II 314
Pennsylvania, immigration from, southward S3 II 292

Pennsylvania, official map of AV 1899 201
Pennsylvania, western, lawlessness in S3 I 336
Pennsylvania, election for first congress S3 I 38
Pennsylvania genealogies S1-2 I 145
Pennsylvania-German emigration north and west AV 1899 93
Pennsylvania-German genealogy, contributions to S4 I 24, 28, 126
Pennsylvania-German graveyards in the south, tombstone records AV 1899 128
Pennsylvania-German Society S3 III 547; AV 1896 154
Pennsylvania-Germans in the Senece Country AV 1897 1; AV 1898 90, 99, 110, 120, 140
Pennsylvania immigration into New York S1-2 I 312
Pennsylvania in the Mexican War S3 III 499
Pennsylvania inauguration, first S3 III 524
Pennsylvania Military Institute S1-2 I 61, 72, 84
Pennsylvania population, early S4 I 185
Pennsylvania railroad, passenger department of AV 1896 141
Pennsylvania Senate of 1837-38 S3 III 160
Pennsylvania taxables in 1760, 1770, 1780, and 1789 S3 II 464
Pennsylvania volunteer militia, 36th regiment, in the Civil War S3 I 417
Pennsylvania deaths of noted Pennsylvanians S3 III 203, 431
Penter Family AV 1898 248
Pequea, old graveyard at AV 1896 133

Perry, Oliver, presentation of
    medal to S1-2 I 306
Perry County, Middle Ridge
    Church S4 I 267
Perry County, Toboyne Church
    S4 I 276
Perry County, history S1-2 II
    41
Perry's Battle Flag AV 1897 90,
    156-158
Perry's Victory, illumination in
    honor of S3 I 477
Perschinger Family AV 1899 205
Persohn Family AV 1898 248
Personn Family S3 II 193
Peter Family AV 1898 248
Peter's Mountain Road S1-2 I 15;
    S3 II 302
Petersen, William, poem by S1-2
    II 346
Peterson, Reverend John Diedrich
    S1-2 I 115
Petry Family AV 1899 205
Pettigrew Family S3 I 243
"Pextang to Menakasie" S1-2 II
    113
Pflantz Family AV 1898 248
Pfatticher Family AV 1899 205
Pfoutz Family S3 II 322
Philadelphia Conference, preachers
    of S4 II 12
Philbert Family AV 1899 205
Philips Family AV 1899 206
Philipsburg, historical sketch of
    AV 1898 3
Phipps Family, inquiry concern-
    ing AV 1897 189; AV 1899 151,
    189
Pickering Family AV 1896 180
Piercel Family AV 1897 323
Piersol Family AV 1898 79
"Pine Ford" S3 II 468
Pine Spring, legend of AV 1896
    191

Pinkerton Family S4 I 142
Pioneer preachers AV 1898 102
Piper, Margaret S4 I 80
Piper Family S4 I 142; AV 1897
    35
Piquet, M., and M. Saugrain, in
    the Ohio Valley S3 II 470
Pittsburgh, census of, in 1810 S3
    II 132
Pittsburgh, old forts at AV 1898
    28
Placing Family AV 1899 210
Plattner Family AV 1899 206
Play Bill, an old S1-2 II 79
Plumer, Margaret Lowrey S4 II 57
Plunket, Dr. William S3 III 153,
    210, 289, 321
Poe, Edgar Allen, Pennsylvania
    ancestry S4 I 106
Poe, Elizabeth Potter AV 1898
    186
Poe, Captain James S1-2 I 473
Poe Family AV 1898 177
Poer Family S3 II 322
Poffenberger Family AV 1898 65
Politics in 1799 S1-2 I 364
Politics in 1841 S4 I 5
Polk Family AV 1899 194
Pollock, John, note S1-2 II 305
Pollack, Margaret O'Brien AV
    1896 153
Pollack, Oliver, of Silver Spring
    S1-2 I 475; S1-2 II 29, 274
Pollock Family S4 I 142
Pollock Family of Silver Spring
    S1-2 II 73
Pontius Family AV 1898 30
Poor Family S3 III 507
Poorman Family S3 I 253
Pope Family AV 1897 185
Population, Pennsylvania's early
    S4 I 185
Porter, Elizabeth Parker AV 1898
    141

Porter, Samuel S4 I 98
Porter Family S3 I 254; S4 I 95,
   142; S4 II 97; AV 1897 121; AV
   1899 176
Porterfield Family S3 III 195
Postage, the originator of cheap
   S3 II 26
Postage rates, old time S4 I 212
Postal facilities in 1742 S3 II 278
Postlethwaite Family S3 II 451;
   S4 I 19
Pott Family AV 1900 187
Potter, General James, death of
   S3 II 88
Potter, John S3 III 222
Potter and Patterson Families
   S1-2 II 304
Potter Family S3 II 203
Potts, Stacy S1-2 I 453
Potts Family S3 I 254
Powell Family S3 III 565; AV 1896
   60; AV 1899 299
Powell's Valley, Bauerman's
   Church S3 II 284, 288
Powell's Valley, Long's Church,
   tombstone records AV 1896
   115
Power Family AV 1899 152, 176
Prather Family S4 I 142
Prehistoric earthworks in Central
   Pennsylvania AV 1899 168
Presbyterian Churches, inquiry
   concerning AV 1900 57
Presbyterian elders, century of
   S4 I 311, 323
Presque Isle Land Co. S1-2 II
   443, 447, 453
Preston Family S3 III 224; S4 I
   247; AV 1899 160
Price Family AV 1896 180
Prices a century ago S3 I 533; S4
   I 100, 103
Prices in Paxtang 130 years ago
   S1-2 II 207

Prices in 1766 S3 II 108
Prices in 1808 S3 II 70
Prices of wearing material 130
   years ago S1-2 II 219
Prices sixty years ago S3 I 346
Printers, old S3 I 243
Procter, Thomas S3 III 108; AV
   1899 224
Proundfit, John AV 1896 192
Proundfit Family AV 1896 192
Provincial correspondence AV
   1896 164
Provincial families, some AV
   1896 181
Provincial times, correspondence
   of S3 III 77, 116
Puglia, James Philip S1-2 I 51
Pumroy Family AV 1899 68
Purdy Family S3 II 341
Putt, Dr. Edward J. S3 III 237

Q

Quickel Family AV 1900 80
Quiggle Family AV 1900 80
Quigley Family of Cumberland
   Valley AV 1898 264

R

Radebach Family AV 1899 206
Rahm Family S3 III 260
Railroad, first in U. S. S3 III 235
Railroad cars, first at Harrisburg
   S1-2 I 460
Railroad reminiscences of 50
   years ago AV 1899 18
Ralston, Andrew, of Big Spring,
   land grant of S1-2 II 91
Ralston. David, family of S1-2 II
   92
Ralston Family S1-2 II 316; AV
   1896 87
Ramberger Family S3 II 175; AV
   1898 249

Ramsey, Thomas S1-2 I 363
Ramsey Family S4 I 63, 95, 99,
106; S4 II 98; AV 1896 37
Rank Family S4 I 119
Ranke Family S4 II 245
Rankin traitors S1-2 I 235
Rathform Family AV 1898 249
Rauch Family AV 1898 249
Raudenbusch, Ulrich, note S1-2
II 327
Rawn, Charles Coatsworth S1-2
II 225
Rea, John S4 I 122
Rea Family AV 1899 112
Read, Adam S1-2 II 226
Read, Adam, documents relating
to S3 I 430, 440, 453
Read, Collinson S3 III 116
Read, James S3 III 115
Read Family AV 1900 58
Redick, David S4 II 62; AV 1898
21
Redsecker Family S3 III 531
Reed, Captain John, company of,
in the Revolution S1-2 II 81
Reed Family S3 I 22, 394, 527; S3
II 323; S4 II 86; AV 1896 115;
AV 1897 152; AV 1900 35, 86
Reeder's painting of John Harris
AV 1900 36
Reehm Family S3 I 5; S3 III 266
Reel Family S3 II 74
Rees Family S3 I 133
Reesor Family AV 1898 140
Reichart Family AV 1898 250
Reichenbach Family AV 1898 47
Reichert Family AV 1897 34, 68
Reid, Maj. James R., will of AV
1896 66
Reid Family AV 1896 48
Reidenauer Family AV 1898 173,
175
Reigle Family S3 II 282
Reily, Elizabeth Myer S4 I 308

Reily, Dr. George Wolf S4 I 84
Reily, Captain John S1-2 I 365;
S1-2 II 267
Reily, Dr. Luther S1-2 II 226
Reim Family AV 1898 46
Reimer Family AV 1898 47
Rein Family AV 1898 249
Reinoehl Family AV 1898 249
Reisch Family S3 II 231
Reiss Family AV 1900 35
Renick, George, land grant to
AV 1899 83
Renick Family of Paxtang S3 II
469
Renick's Island S3 I 200
Reninger Family S3 II 202
Rennie Family AV 1899 226
Renno Family AV 1899 206
Retrospect, 1791-1891 S4 I 20
Reuter Family AV 1898 249
Revolution, application for pension
by a soldier of the AV 1899 238
Revolution, battles of S4 I 244
Revolution, brevet military rank
in S3 II 314
Revolution, correspondence of
S1-2 I 145; S4 I 27, 30, 47; AV
1898 17
Revolution, documents relating to
S3 II 49, 142, 280, 369, 442, 448,
459, 465
Revolution, grist mill of the S4 I
173
Revolution, incident of S3 I 31
Revolution, Lancaster Battalions
in S3 III 27, 546
Revolution, Lancaster County pen-
sioners S4 I 81
Revolution, militia of S3 II 42
Revolution, Millersburg and the
S4 I 41
Revolution, a muster roll of AV
1896 72
Revolution, non-associators in S3

II 373

Revolution, notes AV 1900 134, 146, 152, 159, 166, 171, 186, 199, 210, 218, 222, 224

Revolution, officers from Lancaster County in S1-2 I 459

Revolution, papers relating to S3 I 42, 51, 61, 78, 164, 250, 395, 404, 406; S4 II 43

Revolution, payrolls of S4 I 203, 213; AV 1898 85, 125

Revolution, Pennsylvania Navy in S3 II 314

Revolution, Pennsylvania Quakers in S1-2 I 189

Revolution, pensioners of, in Cumberland County AV 1898 . 191

Revolution, pensioners of, in Westmoreland County AV 1898 283

Revolution, soldiers in S1-2 I 7, 22, 26, 141, 149, 177, 259, 349, 384, 399, 424, 450, 474, 483; S3 I 78; S4 I 9, 65, 98, 149, 157, 160, 173, 175, 304; S4 II 55, 63; AV 1896 108, 118; AV 1900 118, 126, 127, 166, 181, 199, 210, 218, 224

Revolution, worthies of S3 II 49, 350; S3 III 490, 493, 496, 501, 509, 532; S4 II 37, 46, 147, 241, 262

Revolutionary heroes AV 1900 81, 166

Revolutionary heroes living in 1832 S1-2 II 422

Revolutionary officers from Pennsylvania who died in service AV 1899 127

Revolutionary relic, how it was lost AV 1899 49

Revolutionary soldiers, deaths S3 III 98

Reyer Family AV 1898 249

Reynolds, William S3 III 223

Reynolds Family S4 I 130; AV 1898 226, 249; AV 1899 58, 171

Rheese Family S4 II 329

Rheumatism, cider, a cure for S1-2 I 215

Rhoads Family S3 III 115

Richardson Family S4 I 97, 100, 102

Richart Family S4 I 119

Richey Family AV 1899 210

Rickert Family S3 I 259

Riddell, Mrs. Mary S4 I 92

Riddle Family S3 I 1

Riegel Family S3 I 553; AV 1899 206

Riehl Family AV 1899 206

Rieper, Jacob S4 I 107

Rife Family S3 II 1

Rigg Family AV 1899 157, 159

Ring Family AV 1896 180

Ripley Family AV 1899 189

Ripper, John G. S1-2 I 481

Rippeth Family S3 I 22, 254

Ritner Family S3 I 523

Ritschart Family AV 1899 214

Ritscher Family S4 I 113

Road account, an old S3 I 209

Road from Harris' Ferry to the Potomac S3 III 29

Road from Walnut Bottom to the Susquehanna in 1741 S1-2 II 1

Road petitions, old time S3 II 352, 355, 363

Roads, old S3 III 12, 440

Roan, Governor Archibald, note S1-2 II 93, 357

Roan, Reverend John, Congregation of S3 I 338, 348, 361

Roan, Reverend John, itinerary of S3 I 399

Roan, Reverend John, marriages by, 1754-1775 S1-2 II 7, 56

Roan, Reverend John, notitia from

account books of S3 I 455
Roan, Reverend John, obituary of S3 II 441
Roan, Reverend John, of Derry S1-2 I 366
Roan, Reverend John, of Derry; subscription book S1-2 I 458
Roan, Reverend John, salary due at death S3 I 365
Roan, Reverend John, will of S1-2 II 341
Roan Family S1-2 II 93
Robb Family AV 1897 82
Roberdeau, General Daniel, claim of S3 III 428
Roberts, Jonathan, of Montgomery, note S1-2 II 189
Robertson Family S3 I 255
Robinson, Captain Thomas, rangers of AV 1900 186
Robinson Family S3 I 8; AV 1896 139
Rocky Springs Church S4 II 98-108
Roddy, James, notes S1-2 I 283, 440
Rodgers, Captain James, company of, in the Revolution S1-2 II 54
Rodgers, Reverend William S3 II 341
Rodgers Family AV 1899 171
Roeger Family AV 1899 206
Rogers Family S4 II 173, 197
Rogers Family of Hanover S3 III 226; S4 II 273, 291
Rohm Family AV 1899 206, 214
Rolling Mills, early S1-2 I 439
Roop, Mrs. Lydia S4 I 66
Roop Family S3 I 512, 814
Root, William S4 I 317
Rosbrugh, Jane Ralston S4 I 295
Rosbrugh Family S4 I 310
Rosenberger Family AV 1898 249
Ross, Robert James S1-2 II 406

Ross Family AV 1897 23, 54; AV 1898 41, 60; AV 1900 70
Rost Family AV 1899 206
Roth Family AV 1898 174
Rothrock Family S4 II 245, 246, 250
Roumfort, Charles E. AV 1900 45
"Round Top" S3 I 2
Rowan Family S3 III 241; S4 I 30, 66
Royer Family S4 I 12
Rudeisel Family AV 1898 249
Rueger Family AV 1898 248
Runk Family S3 II 283
Runkle Family graveyard, tombstone records AV 1899 51
Russell Family S3 I 255
Ruth Family AV 1898 248
Rutherford, Dr. Hiram AV 1900 78
Rutherford, Captain John, company of S1-2 I 399
Rutherford, John A. S4 I 65
Rutherford, John B. S4 I 129
Rutherford, Dr. Levi S1-2 II 406
Rutherford, Samuel S4 I 93
Rutherford, William S1-2 II 226; S4 I 83
Rutherford, William Swan S4 II 226
Rutherford Family record S1-2 I 121
Rutherford golden wedding S3 III 296
Rutherford memorial AV 1898 37
Ryan Family AV 1899 171

S

St. Clair, Phoebe Bayard S4 I 282
St. Clair Family S4 II 318; AV 1897 55, 62, 65, 68, 80; AV 1899 68
St. Clair's defeat, officers killed

at S3 III 564
St. James Church, Lancaster,
    baptisms AV 1900 202, 206, 214
St. James Church, Lancaster,
    marriage records AV 1897 3,
    11, 16, 19, 25, 27, 37, 42, 51
St. Johns, Berrysburg S4 II 167
St. Mary's Church at Lancaster
    AV 1896 131
St. Peters, Middletown S3 I 222
Sallade, Simon S1-2 I 206; S3 I
    207
Salona (Pennsylvania), tombstone
    records AV 1896 199
Salter Family AV 1899 214
Sands Family AV 1900 59
"Sangaree" S3 I 294
Sankey, Reverend Richard S1-2 II
    198
Sankey Family, inquiry concerning
    AV 1900 68
Sauer, George S4 I 105
Sauer, John S4 I 105
Saugrain, M. and M. Piquet in the
    Ohio Valley S3 II 470
Sawyer Family S1-2 I 88; S3 II
    344; S3 III 176; AV 1899 181
Sawyers, Captain James S3 II 12
Sayford, Joseph, reminiscences of
    AV 1898 34
Sayre Family S3 II 444
Schade Family AV 1899 207
Schaefer Family S3 II 208
Schaeffer Family S3 III 260; AV
    1899 207
Schaffner Family S3 I 500
Schaick Family S3 II 209
Schaller Family S4 II 251
Schallery Family AV 1898 250
Schanbacher Family S4 II 108
Schank Family S4 II 251
Schans Family S4 II 251
Scharff Family AV 1899 207
Schauer Family AV 1899 207

Schautz Family S3 II 194
Scheffel Family AV 1898 46
Schell Family S3 II 246; AV 1899
    207
Schieble Family S3 II 194
Schindel Family AV 1898 258
Schirmann Family AV 1899 207
Schlayer, Andrew S4 I 89
Schley Family AV 1899 77
Schlosser, George Ernest S3 III 188
Schlosser Family S3 III 188; S4 II
    250; AV 1898 256
Schlotterbeck Family AV 1898 258
Schmaal Family AV 1898 256
Schmeltzer Family S3 II 237
Schmidt Family AV 1898 257; AV
    1899 207
Schminkey, Dr. I. S. AV 1900 46
Schneider Family AV 1899 208
Schnock Family AV 1896 256
Schnug Family AV 1896 250
Schoch Family AV 1900 121
"Schonbrunn" S4 I 266
Schoolmasters, old-time S1-2 II
    357
Schools, early S1-2 I 33; S1-2 II
    470
Schools, free S3 II 301
Schools and school teachers, old
    S3 I 518
Schopp Family AV 1899 208
Schott Family S4 I 23
Schroff Family AV 1899 208
Schropp Family of Northumber-
    land S3 III 158
Schuler Family AV 1899 212
Schumacher Family S4 II 245
Schwab Family AV 1898 256
Schwarz Family AV 1898 47
Scotland, badges of the clans S1-2
    I 238
Scott, Josiah, family of S4 I 138
Scott, Captain Matthew S4 II 177;
    AV 1899 3

Scott Family S3 II 214, 344, 438, 455; S3 III 131, 136; S4 I 95, 99, 136; AV 1897 9; AV 1900 14, 74, 121
Scraps of local history S1-2 I 418
Scroggs, John A., of Beaver, note S1-2 II 189
Scroggs Family AV 1900 100
Seager Family S3 III 557
Seal, Jacob S4 I 73
Seal Family S3 I 256; S3 III 152
Sealsfield, Charles S4 I 85
Seaman Family AV 1899 207
Second Street extension in 1805 S1-2 II 141
Seebolt Family AV 1898 43
Seehale Family S3 II 245
Sehner Family S3 II 452
Seiler, Daniel W. S4 I 87
Seiler, Henry S1-2 I 355
Seiler Family S4 II 247
Selin, Major Anthony AV 1896 203; AV 1897 115
Semple Family S3 II 324, 466; S4 I 66
Senier Family S3 II 194
Senseman Family AV 1899 176
Sensendorfer Family AV 1898 218
Seruniyattha, or Half-King S1-2 II 78
Settlers, arrival of early S1-2 I 412
Settlers, early, in Armstrong's Valley S3 I 78
Settlers, early warrants to S3 II 188
Settlers, life of S3 I 496; S3 III 511
Shaeffer Family S3 I 412
Shaffner, Philip S4 II 183
Shaffner Family S3 I 500
Shannon Family AV 1897 220
Sharer Family S4 I 62
Sharon, Reverend James R. S4 I 130, 134, 147
Sharon Family S4 I 130, 134

Sharp Family AV 1896 73, 86, 87; AV 1897 8
Sharpe Family AV 1896 143; AV 1897 46
Shaw Family S3 II 343
Shawanese Indians S3 I 303
Sheaffer Family AV 1900 59
Shearer Family AV 1899 153
Shearman's Valley, original name of S312 II 63; S3 II 204
Shee Family S3 III 372
Sheesly Family AV 1896 87
Sheetz Family S3 I 256
Shell's Church, tombstone records S3 III 67
Shenk Family S3 II 78
Shepherd Family AV 1899 153
Sherer, Captain Joseph S3 I 247
Sherer, Captain Joseph, company of S1-2 I 384
Sherer Family S3 III 501
Shields Family AV 1899 68
"Shin-Plasters" S3 II 165
Shippen Family S4 II 329; AV 1896 181-186
Shippensburg, early settlement of S1-2 II 2
Shoch, John S1-2 I 366
Shockley, Christopher, complaint of S3 II 417
Shoemaker, George J. AV 1898 293
Shoop, Captain John P., militia company of S3 I 7
Shoop Family AV 1896 86
Shoop's Church records S3 I 179, 186, 194, 202, 368, 371, 377, 385
Shope, Dr. David, personal recollections of S3 II 71
Shope, Dr. Jacob AV 1898 293
Shope Family S3 II 74
Shott Family S3 I 256
Shourler, Valentine S1-2 II 406
Showers Family AV 1897 233

Shrom Family AV 1900 126
Shulze, Governor J. Andrew S1-2
    I 247
Shuster Family S3 II 1
Shwab Family S3 II 343
Siechele Family AV 1898 250
Sigler Family S4 I 258; AV 1900
    173
Silver Family of Silver Spring
    S1-2 I 465
Silver Lake, graveyard at S4 I 235
Simmons, Samuel, family of AV
    1897 187
Simmons, Colonel Seneca G. S1-2
    I 337, 367
Simmons Family S4 II 256
Simons Family S3 II 343
Simonton, Dr. William S1-2 I 367
Simonton Family AV 1900 52
Simpson, John S1-2 I 1, 139, 368;
    AV 1896 171
Simpson, Captain John, neighbors
    of, in 1776 S3 II 180
Simpson, Margaret Murray S4 I
    306
Simpson Family of Paxtang S3 III
    209; S4 I 44
Singer Family S3 I 257; AV 1899
    112; AV 1900 222
Singhaas Family AV 1898 257
Skanawati, leader of the Iroquois
    S4 I 184
Skelton Family AV 1896 141
Slavery in 1795 S3 I 445
Slaymaker Family S4 I 127, 138;
    S4 II 321
Sloan, Alexander S4 I 315
Sloan, "Cinquas", inquiry concern-
    ing S1-2 I 18
Sloan, Robert S4 I 313
Sloan Family AV 1899 14, 68, 210,
    226
Sloan Family of Hanover S1-2 II
    174

Slocum Family AV 1900 189
Slough Family S1-2 II 404
Small Family of York S3 III 52
Smith, Charles, of Sunbury AV
    1897 12
Smith, Henry, note S1-2 II 305
Smith, Isaac AV 1896 172
Smith, John S3 III 218
Smith, John R. C., note S1-2 II 190
Smith, Colonel Matthew S1-2 II
    467; S3 I 174; S3 III 441
Smith, Robert AV 1896 172
Smith, Reverend Robert, of Pequea
    S1-2 II 77
Smith Family S3 I 257; S3 II 79;
    S4 I 89, 102; AV 1896 139, 185;
    AV 1897 233; AV 1898 28, 211;
    AV 1899 62, 139, 171
Smithers Family AV 1900 36
Smolnikar, Andrew D. AV 1899 122
Smull, John Augustus S1-2 I 25
Snaketown S1-2 I 1, 10, 19, 41, 70
Snavely Family S3 III 558
Snively Family S3 III 218
Snoddy Family S3 I 342
Snodgrass, Reverend James S1-2
    I 368, 371
Snodgrass, Reverend James, re-
    miniscences of S3 III 27
Snodgrass, Reverend William Da-
    vis S1-2 I 25
Snodgrass Family S3 II 144, 343;
    S4 I 100; AV 1900 22
Snoke Family S3 II 206.
Snow storm of 1831 S4 I 93
Snowden, Reverend Nathaniel K.,
    Paxtang's subscription to S1-2
    II 279
Snug Family S3 I 342
Snyder, Mrs. Barbara Ann S4 I 86
Snyder, Governor Simon, note S3 I
    534
Snyder Family S3 I 343, 534
Soldiers' Rest S3 II 395

"Soldier's Tale, The", the charac-
    ters in S1-2 I 54, 397
Somer Family AV 1899 208
Songs of other days AV 1900 178,
    184
Sox Family AV 1899 139
Spangenberg, Bishop, journal of, in
    1745 S1-2 I 117
Spayd Family S3 II 494; S3 III 12
Spears Family AV 1898 131
Sperry Family S4 II 259
Spidle Family AV 1896 87
Sponsler Family S3 III 66
Sprecher Family AV 1898 257, 258
Sprecker Family S3 II 183, 246
Sproat, Maria Thompson AV 1898
    172
Sproul Family AV 1897 144
Spyker, Colonel Henry AV 1897
    19, 184
Spyker Family AV 1897 184; AV
    1898 171
Squirrels, extermination of S4 I 45
Stage coaches, early S3 II 161
Staging, the days of S3 I 207
Stambaugh, Samuel C. S1-2 I 247
Stamp Act of 1797 S4 II 251
"Star-Spangled Banner" AV 1897
    107
State, a new S3 II 117
States, nicknames of S3 II 178
Stauffer Family S4 I 305
Steckley, Matthew S4 I 123
Steckley Family S3 II 342
Stedman Family S3 II 143
Steedman, General James B. S4 I
    10
Steel, James, letter of S1-2 I 8
Steel, Reverend John, grave of
    S1-2 II 296
Steel Family S3 I 344; S4 II 312;
    AV 1900 195
Steele, James S1-2 II 407, 423
Steele, Colonel John S3 II 269

Steele Family AV 1897 126; AV
    1898 180
Steger Family S3 II 238
Stehman Family S4 I 66
Stenography, old time AV 1900 209
Stephen Family S3 II 342
Stephenson Family AV 1897 123
Sterret and Green S1-2 II 46
Sterret Family S3 I 344; S3 III
    204; AV 1899 162
Steuart, Thomas, home of AV
    1897 157
Stevens, Thaddeus, and his "Tape
    Worm" Railroad AV 1899 3, 6,
    11
Stevensburg, Virginia S1-2 I 490
Stewart, Andrew, of Paxtang S1-2
    I 12, 43
Stewart, Ben, execution of S4 I 289
Stewart, John, of Tuscarora AV
    1896 197
Stewart, Deborah McClenahan AV
    1899 2
Stewart, Captain Lazarus S1-2 I
    369
Stewart, Captain Lazarus, ances-
    tors of S1-2 II 127, 197
Stewart, Captain Lazarus, family
    of S3 II 45
Stewart, Captain Lazarus, notes
    concerning S1-2 II 442
Stewart, Margaret Forster AV
    1897 157
Stewart, Martha Espy AV 1896 49
Stewart, William AV 1898 185
Stewart Family S1-2 I 2, 94; S3 I
    354, 461, 492; S3 II 45, 144, 160,
    323; S3 III 442, 467, 489; S4 I
    30, 100, 151, 170; AV 1897 8;
    AV 1898 70, 185
Stewart Family, inquiry concern-
    ing S1-2 II 88
Stewart Family of Cumberland
    Valley S3 III 442; AV 1899 38, 22?

Stewart Family of Donegal S3 III 467, 489
Stewart Family of Hanover S1-2 I 31
Stilwell Family S3 II 44
Stine Family S4 II 43
Stober Family AV 1898 256
Stoever, Reverend John Casper AV 1896 2
Stoever, Reverend John Casper, baptisms by AV 1896 3, 10, 16, 22, 27, 33, 39, 44, 51, 55, 56, 61, 68, 74
Stoever, Reverend John Casper, marriages by AV 1896 80, 88, 96, 104, 111
Stoever Family AV 1898 258
Stony Creek, inquiry concerning S3 I 78
"Stophen", an abbreviation for Christopher S1-2 I 32
Stover Family S3 II 220, 231
Stoy, Reverend William, letter of S1-2 II 314
Strain Family S3 I 344
Straub, Andrew, note AV 1896 175; AV 1897 41
Strauss Family AV 1899 212
Straw Family S3 II 194
"Straw Jacket, a confab with" S1-2 I 242
Strawbridge Family S4 I 79; AV 1897 47
Strebich Family AV 1898 257
Stroecher Family AV 1898 256, 257
Stroh Family AV 1896 170; AV 1898 257, 258
Stroh-Schneider Family AV 1899 212
Stroh's graveyard AV 1896 170
Strubig Family S4 II 245
Struman Family S3 II 244
Stuart Family S3 I 493; S3 II 323;

AV 1898 250; AV 1899 224
Stuckey Family S3 II 238
Sturgeon, Daniel S3 III 48
Sturgeon Family S3 II 324; S4 I 4
Sturgeon Family reunion AV 1899 171
Sullivan County, contributions to history S4 I 220, 225, 237, 239, 244; S4 II 71, 87, 113, 126, 129, 137, 143, 150, 161, 164, 173, 184, 189, 195, 203, 212, 219, 225, 232, 235, 255, 259, 270, 274, 309, 318, 324, 338
Sullivan County, water-shed of S3 II 472
Sullivan expedition of 1779 AV 1899 239
Summerville Family AV 1899 170
Sunbury, tombstone records S3 III 230
Susquehanna and Delaware Companies S4 I 186
Susquehanna River AV 1897 87
Susquehanna River, early exploration of S1-2 I 390
Susquehanna River, early settler on the AV 1899 83
Susquehanna River, early surveys on the S3 I 484
Susquehanna River, ferries over the S1-2 I 106
Susquehanna River, first skates on S3 II 319
Susquehanna River, floods on the S3 I 491
Susquehanna River, improvement of S4 I 139
Susquehanna River, islands in the S3 III 311
Susquehanna River, navigation of the S1-2 II 275, 280, 348; S3 III 16
Susquehanna River, origin of the name of the S3 II 385

Susquehanna River, west
  branch AV 1900 136, 142, 149,
  154
Susquehanna River, who first
  descended the S3 III 221
Susquehanna River, region, old
  map of S3 II 37
Sutherland, Joel B., of Philadel-
  phia, note S1-2 II 189
Swab, Eli AV 1898 25
Swan, Richard S1-2 II 450
Swan Family record S1-2 I 154
Swatara, early settlers on the
  S1-2 I 412; S1-2 II 179
Swatara, fords over the S1-2 II
  201
Swatara, ghosts of the S1-2 II 367
Swatara, old time ruins in S3 III
  541
Swatara region, trip through the
  S4 II 200, 206, 216
Swenk Family S4 I 113
Swetland, Hannah Tiffany AV 1898
  237
Swift Family AV 1899 153
Swineford Family AV 1896 170
Swiss settlers, early AV 1900 121
Switzer's land S1-2 II 360
Swope, Gilbert E., of Newville AV
  1899 95
Sytez Family AV 1896 122

                    T

"Tailor's goose will never fly"
  (poem) S3 I 454
Talbot, Jeremiah S3 III 223
Talleyrand at Bellefonte S4 I 85
"Tape Worm" AV 1899 3, 6, 11
Tappen Family AV 1899 109
Tasistro, note S1-2 II 160
Tatamy S3 II 359
Tate, Elizabeth, note S1-2 II 305
Tate, Reverend Joseph S4 I 248

Tate Family S3 II 144; S4 I 63, 248
Tavern keepers in 1783 AV 1900
  167
Tavern licenses 50 years ago AV
  1896 120
Taxes, collection of excise S1-2
  II 334
Taylor, Bessie, an Indian captive
  S1-2 II 330
Taylor Family S3 I 345, 476; S3 II
  467; S3 III 502; S4 II 260; AV
  1899 154; AV 1900 52
Teedyuscung, anecdotes of S3 III
  196
Teedyuscung, notices of S3 III 551
Telegraph, magnetic first, at Har-
  risburg S1-2 I 253
Telegraph dispatch, the first S1-2
  I 458
Telegraph message, first over the
  Allegheny Mountains S1-2 II 63
Temperance societies, early S4 I
  1, 6
Templeton, Robert S1-2 I 302
Templeton Family S3 III 168
"Ten miles to T'" AV 1898 53
Thanksgiving days in Pennsylvania
  S3 II 306
Theater and circus in the long ago
  S3 III 199, 228
Thomas, Ursula Muller S4 II 306
Thomas Family, notes S3 I 33; S3
  II 160; AV 1898 231; AV 1899
  153, 212
Thome, John S4 I 6
Thome Family AV 1898 53
Thompson, Colonel James S3 III
  118
Thompson, Nathan S3 III 122
Thompson, Colonel Robert S3 II
  121
Thompson, General William S4 I
  253
Thompson, Captain William, note

S1-2 II 309

Thompson Family S3 II 344, 422;
    S3 III 482; S4 I 89, 253; AV 1898
    185, 279; AV 1899 63, 101; AV
    1900 100

Thomson, Hannah Harrison AV
    1898 136

Thomson Family AV 1897 54; AV
    1899 112

Thornton Family S3 III 169

Thortheuer Family AV 1899 212

Tilghman, James, letter of S3 II 70

"Tinian", residence of Colonel
    James Burd S1-2 II 339

Tintorff Family AV 1896 86

Tioga County S4 I 67, 79

Tobey, William Carrell S1-2 I 239

Toboyne Church S4 I 276

Tod, Honorable John S1-2 II 407;
    AV 1900 39, 47

Todd Family AV 1896 221

"Tokens" used in churches S1-2 I
    5

Toll-gate, the last S3 I 547

Tomatoes, their first use S3 I 355

Tombstone records S3 I 9, 13, 19,
    24, 108, 148, 222, 233, 251, 313,
    371, 375, 385, 402, 409, 414, 423,
    428, 435, 438, 497, 508, 511, 520,
    526, 528, 536, 543, 548, 556, 558;
    S3 II 41, 112, 368, 478; S3 III 34,
    57, 67, 110, 230, 261, 268, 270,
    271, 274, 276, 284, 312, 344, 358,
    362, 368, 380, 383, 386, 401, 450;
    S4 I 11, 114, 115, 123, 235, 267,
    276; S4 II 80, 106, 167, 207, 221,
    216, 254; AV 1896 7, 67, 115,
    119, 133, 170, 199, 218; AV 1897
    46, 79, 102, 115, 117, 127, 147,
    161, 164, 167, 177, 180, 207, 218,
    219; AV 1898 23, 31, 43, 61, 66,
    74, 81, 86, 93, 108, 112, 121, 146,
    147, 160, 169, 206, 207, 221, 286,
    296, 301; AV 1899 15, 22, 25, 45,

51, 55, 64, 69, 74, 80, 89, 113, 118,
    128, 147, 169, 173, 204, 210, 211,
    220, 231

Toot Family S3 I 29

Torrence Family AV 1899 138

Tory, a Paxtang boy's definition of
    S1-2 II 351

"Tory Outlaw", Simon Girty, The
    S1-2 II 66

Toryism at Middletown S3 I 441

Traill, Elizabeth Grotz S4 II 4

Transportation a half century ago
    S1-2 II 284

Trent, James, note S1-2 II 305

Trent, Captain William and the
    Indian traders of 1763 S1-2 II
    31, 37

Trent, Captain William S1-2 II 4,
    12, 18

Trenton and Princeton, officers at
    S1-2 I 459

Trewick, Walter S4 I 83

Trimble, James, note S1-2 I 6, 305

Trimble Family AV 1897 8

Tripp Family S4 II 277

Trissler Family AV 1898 47

Troester Family AV 1899 212

Trotter, James, letter to Colonel
    Burd S3 II 91

Troxel Family AV 1896 86

Tulpehocken Church, the little AV
    1899 185, 190, 205, 212, 216

"Turkey Island" in the Susquehan-
    na S1-2 II 364

Turner Family, note S3 I 26

Turnpike order, an old S3 II 165

Tuscarawa County (Ohio), early
    Pennsylvania settlers in S4 I
    279

Tuscarawas, the S4 I 274

Tweed Family S3 II 144

U

Uhler Family S3 III 513; AV

1898 258
Ulrich Family AV 1898 259, 280
Umberger Family AV 1898 258
Umholtz Family S1-2 I 209; AV 1900 171
Umstead Family, inquiry concerning S1-2 II 88, 275
Underground railroad S3 II 325
Underwood, John S3 III 217
Union Deposit, tombstone records at S3 I 402
United Brethren, origin of the name of S3 II 177
United Brethren conference, first S3 III 374
United companies of Illinois and Wabash AV 1897 85
U. S. Army register from 1775-1879 S1-2 II 30, 40
U. S. Tax in 1813 S3 II 371.
University of Pennsylvania, graduates of S1-2 I 330
Unruh Family AV 1899 212
Updegraff Family, inquiry concerning AV 1899 152
Upper Paxtang assessment, 1778 S1-2 I 271
Upper Paxtang in the Revolution S1-2 I 177
Urich Family AV 1899 176, 212
Urie Family, inquiry concerning S3 III 179; S4 I 239; AV 1899 226

V

Valentine Family AV 1896 32
Vallerchamp Family AV 1897 40
Valley Forge, sufferings at S3 II 459
Van Beaver Family, inquiry concerning S3 I 16
Van Beuren Family AV 1899 154
Van Camp, John S4 II 32
Vance Family S3 I 356; AV 1897 65

Vandergrift burial records AV 1899 55
Vandike Family AV 1899 154
Van Dyke Family S3 I 356
Van Gundy Family AV 1900 195
Van Hoff, Reverend A. H., baptismal register of S3 III 451, 456, 457, 460, 462
Vanhorn Family AV 1897 102
Vanlear Family S1-2 II 416
Vaughn Family AV 1899 226
Verbeke, William K. AV 1898 52
Vetter Family AV 1898 45
Victor belong the spoils, to the AV 1897 93
Virginia Genealogies S4 I 80
Vogel Family S3 II 207
Vollmar Family AV 1899 212
Volz Family AV 1898 46
Vondersmith Family AV 1898 180
Vonder Weide Family AV 1898 261
Von Phul, Henry S4 II 129
Von Porta Family AV 1898 47

W

Wabash, United companies of Illinois AV 1897 85
Waddell Family AV 1899 161
Wade Family AV 1899 226
Wagenseller Family AV 1897 214
Wagner Family S1-2 II 345; AV 1898 261, 262; AV 1899 212, 213
Wagoning in ye old time AV 1899 229
Walborn Family AV 1900 35
Walker, Captain Thomas S1-2 I 370
Walker Family S3 I 357; S3 II 204, 460; S3 III 495; S4 I 130; S4 II 148; AV 1898 220; AV 1899 160
"Walking Purchase" S3 II 167
Wall, Garret, diary of AV 1900 165

Wallace, Captain Benjamin S1-2 I
379, 458
Wallace, Irwin M. S4 I 182
Wallace, James S1-2 II 227
Wallace, Samuel S1-2 II 292, 329
Wallace, William S1-2 I 372; S1-2
II 456
Wallace Family S1-2 I 120; S3 II
160; S3 III 34; AV 1897 233
Wallis, Lydia Hollingsworth S4 I
301
Walmers Church, tombstone rec-
ords S4 II 207, 216
Walnut Hill, residence of Colonel
James Crouch S1-2 II 339
Wampum S3 I 288
War history as written in 1887 S3
II 437
War of 1812-1814 AV 1900 163
War of 1812-1814, Alleghany Coun-
ty in AV 1900 163
War of 1812-1814, Franklin County
in S1-2 I 448
War of 1812-1814, Harrisburg
Volunteers in S1-2 I 280
War of 1812-1814, muster roll of
AV 1896 147
War of 1812-1814, pensioners of
S4 II 262
Ward, John Q. A., ancestors of
S1-2 I 223
Ward Family AV 1899 85
Warford, Joseph, will of AV 1897
117
Warrington Friends' Meeting House
AV 1897 189
Warrington Friends' Meeting House,
tombstone records AV 1899 220
Washington, George, at Harrisburg
in 1794 S1-2 II 52
Washington, George, death of S3 I
452
Washington, George, first foreign
person named for S3 I 8

Washington correspondence, un-
published S4 I 36, 38, 42, 50, 53,
56, 58
Washington County, worthies AV
1896 191
Washington's aides AV 1898 86
Washington's death, effect of S3 II
153
Washington's itinerary in 1794
S1-2 I 224
Washington's rebuke to Colonel
Moylan S1-2 II 353
Waterbury, Isaac S1-2 II 409
Watson Family S3 II 345; S4 I 243;
AV 1897 203, 204
Watts, General Frederick, of the
Revolution S1-2 II 74
Watts, Jean Murray S4 II 19
Watts Family AV 1899 154
Waugh, Beverly Roberts S1-2 II
228
Waugh, Reverend Samuel S3 III
413
Waugh Family AV 1898 8
Wayne, General Anthony, life story
of, by Dr. Stille S4 I 196
Wayne, Mary Penrose AV 1898 177
Wearing material, prices of 130
years ago S1-2 II 219
Weaver, Captain Martin S1-2 I 229
Weaver, Captain Martin, roll of
company, 1777-1778 AV 1898
125
Weaver Family S3 I 358; AV 1899
15
Weber Family S3 II 209, 238; AV
1896 108, 159; AV 1899 213
Webster Family AV 1899 154
Wegman Family AV 1898 262
Wegner Family AV 1899 262
Weidner Family AV 1900 35
Weir, James Wallace S4 I 315, 324
Weir, John Andrew S4 I 318
Weir, Samuel S1-2 II 228; S4 I 311

Weirick, Jacob S1-2 I 373
Weisbach Family S3 II 221
Weise, Adam S1-2 I 373
Weise Family S1-2 I 288
Weiser, Conrad, advice to his
   countrymen S4 I 32
Weiser, Conrad, and the Indians
   AV 1899 57
Weiser Family AV 1900 36
Weiser's settlement in Pennsyl-
   vania S3 I 462
Weiss Family S3 II 230; AV 1898
   262
Weitzel, Squire John, marriages
   by, from 1806 to 1830 S1-2 II
   176
Weitzel Family AV 1897 165
Wekquitank, annals of AV 1897
   153; AV 1899 123, 129, 134, 140,
   142
Weller Family S4 II 247
Welsh, James, family of S1-2 II
   225
Welsh Family S3 I 358; S3 II 176
Welsh settlers in Lancaster Coun-
   ty AV 1897 224, 231; AV 1898
   54; AV 1899 144
Wenderich Family AV 1899 213
Wenner Family AV 1900 36
Wenrich Church, tombstone rec-
   ords S3 III 110
Wenrich Family AV 1899 213
Wentling, George, hero of 1776
   S4 I 247
Wert, Simon S4 II 183
Wert Family S3 II 246
Wertz Family AV 1899 213
Weschenbach Family AV 1898 262
West Branch, the historic AV
   1898 80
West, Francis of Shearman's
   Valley S1-2 II 87
West Family S3 III 215
Westchester Centennial AV 1900 8

Western Pennsylvania, deaths in
   AV 1898 190
Western Pennsylvania, lawlessness
   in S3 I 336
Western Pennsylvania, marriages
   in AV 1898 190
Western Pennsylvania in 1825 S3
   III 5, 8
Wetherhold Family S3 II 73
Wetherholt Family S4 I 113
Wetterholt, Captain Jacob, company
   of, in 1763 AV 1896 220
Wetterholt, Captain John Nicholas,
   company of, in 1763 AV 1896
   221
Wetzel Family S3 II 403
Weygandt, Maria Agneta Bechtel
   S4 I 309
Weynrich Family AV 1898 262
Weyrich Family AV 1900 194
"Wheelbarrow Man, the" S1-2 II
   397, 423
Whiskey insurrection AV 1898 154,
   161; AV 1900 140
Whiskey insurrection, Dauphin
   County in S1-2 II 130
Whiskey insurrection, papers re-
   lating to S3 II 93, 98, 301
White, Moses, note S1-2 II 305
White, Samuel, history of the war
   of 1812-1814 S3 II 118
White, William, family of S1-2 II
   397
White Church Manor S3 III 510
White Deer Township, Lycoming
   County AV 1899 132
White Family S3 I 358; S3 II 11;
   S4 I 63; AV 1900 195
Whitehill, George S1-2 I 375
Whitehill, Robert S3 III 96
Whitehill Family S3 III 182, 201
Whitesides Family S3 II 152; S4
   I 103
Whitfield at Harris' Ferry S3 I 387

Whitley Family S3 III 495
Whitman Family S3 III 531
Whittaker Family S3 II 345
Wickersham Family S3 I 455
Wiconisco in 1775 S1-2 I 21
Wiconisco Valley, Church grants
   in S3 I 8, 22
Widener Family AV 1899 132
Wier Family, inquiry concerning
   AV 1899 226
Wierman Family AV 1896 139;
   AV 1898 22
Wiestling, Dr. Samuel C. S1-2 I
   374
Wiggins Family S1-2 II 418; S3
   I 22, 111
Wiley Family AV 1899 138; AV
   1900 34
Wilford Family S3 III 163
Wilhelm Family AV 1898 262;
   AV 1899 213
Wilkins Family S3 II 120, 412;
   AV 1900 191
Willard, John Peter S1-2 I 209
Williams, General Edward C. AV
   1900 27
Williams, Reverend Joshua S1-2
   II 409
Williams Family S3 I 359; AV
   1899 201
Williamsburg on Swatara S1-2 I
   243
Williamson Family S4 I 27; AV
   1896 14
Williamsport, Pennsylvania, first
   physician at S4 I 117
Williamsville S1-2 I 263
Willis Family S4 II 122
Willits Family AV 1900 34
Wills murder in 1814 S3 I 310
Willson Family S3 II 145; AV 1900
   151, 194
Wilson, Henry S1-2 I 436
Wilson, Henry, note S1-2 II 126, 210

Wilson, James A. S4 I 67
Wilson, Matthew, note S1-2 I 248
Wilson, Rosanna S4 I 84
Wilson, Thomas S1-2 II 228
Wilson, Thomas Low S1-2 II 229
Wilson Family S1-2 I 97; S3 I 22;
   S3 II 228, 345; S3 III 7, 204, 495;
   S4 I 91; S4 II 171, 261; AV 1896
   54, 126, 210; AV 1899 139; AV
   1900 69, 182
Winagle Family S3 I 112; S4 I 24,
   120
Winchester, Virginia S1-2 I 490,
   495
Winebrenner, Reverend John S1-2
   I 374
Winebrenner, Reverend John, or-
   dination of S1-2 II 50
Wingert Family S3 II 345; AV 1899
   213
Wipff Family AV 1898 262
Wirt Family S4 I 163, 166
Wirtz and Patterson Families
   S1-2 I 59
Wishart Family AV 1899 151
"Wis-que-nes-que", Church of the
   S4 I 77
Witman, Dr. Henry O. S4 I 82
Witmayer Family AV 1899 213
Witmer Family AV 1899 165
Wogan Family AV 1897 92
Wolf Family S3 II 232, 244; AV
   1896 191; AV 1897 189
Wolfarth baptismal record S1-2 II
   358
Wolfarth Family S3 I 360
Wolfersberger Family S3 III 260
Wolff Family S4 II 322
Woltz, Dr. Peter S1-2 II 263, 307
Woltz Family S3 II 44, 111
Wood, Nicholas Bayles S1-2 I 375
Wood Family S1-2 II 134; S4 I 66,
   100; S4 II 299
Woods, Rev. Matthew AV 1900 1

80 INDEX

Woods Family AV 1899 160
Woodside Gap S3 I 11
Work Family S4 I 136
Workman, Benjamin, note S1-2 II 71, 89
Worley, Reverend Daniel S3 III 156
Worrall Family S4 II 123
Wright Family S3 I 360; S3 III 66; AV 1899 154, 170; AV 1900 75, 136
Wunderlich Family AV 1898 171, 262
Wyeth, Francis S1-2 I 247; S4 I 217
Wyeth, John S1-2 I 376
Wyeth, John, comments on Gideon Granger S3 II 87
Wylie Family S3 II 344
Wycoming controversy AV 1896 1, 189
Wycoming historical society AV 1900 145
Wycoming massacre of 1763 S3 III 387
Wycoming massacre of 1763, narrative of S3 III 519
Wycoming Valley, settlement of the S3 III 561

Y

Yeates, Jasper S1-2 I 485
Yeates, Judge, letters from S1-2 II 382
Yeates Family AV 1896 184–186
Yellow fever at Lisburn in 1803 S1-2 II 296
Yoder, Moses, of Oley AV 1899 121
Yoder Family AV 1897 152
York, British prisoners at, in 1781 S3 II 132
York, Moravian records at S4 II 245, 250, 254
York County, troubles of early

settlers in S3 II 145, 155
York Springs, Lutheran Church, tombstone records AV 1899 211
York Springs, Sunnyside Cemetery, tombstone records AV 1899 210
Yorktown (Pennsylvania) S1-2 I 488
Yorktown (Virginia), diary S3 III 368, 376
Yorktown (Virginia), hero of S1-2 II 231
Yorktown (Virginia), letter S1-2 II 231
Yorktown (Virginia), orderly book S1-2 II 247, 255
Yorktown (Virginia) centennial, Pennsylvania at S1-2 II 230
Young, James S4 II 278
Young Family S3 II 246; S4 I 88; AV 1896 220; AV 1898 48, 85; AV 1899 219
Young Family of Hanover S3 III 500

Z

Zechman Family AV 1899 213
Zeisberger, Reverend David, grave of S4 I 262
Zeisberger, Reverend David, tour of, in 1767 S4 I 258, 263, 268, 277
Zeisberger's Spring (Schonbrunn) S4 I 266
Zell Family S4 II 317
Zeller Family AV 1900 34
Zent Family S3 II 72
Zerfass Family AV 1899 176
Zerwe Family AV 1899 213, 214
Zieffle Family AV 1898 262
Ziegel Family AV 1898 21
Ziegler, Major David AV 1897 1
Ziegler, George S1-2 II 229
Ziegler Church graveyard, tombstone records AV 1897 218
Ziegler Family S3 I 361; S3 II 193;